COMMUNICATE TO COMMAND

COMMUNICATE TO COMMAND

LUKE HILL
JAYDEN HENDERSON

Jayden Henderson
To my son, Atticus Henderson

Luke Hill
To the leaders of today and tomorrow

CONTENTS

Introduction   1

Part I: Foundations of Leadership Communication   5

    1 The Heart of Leadership – Empathy   7

    2 Understanding Your Audience   14

    3 Active Listening   24

    4 Nonverbal Communication   30

Part II: Leadership Communication in Action   42

    5 The Role of Public Speaking in Leadership   43

    6 Motivating and Leading Others   53

    7 Coaching and Mentoring   65

    8 Giving and Receiving Feedback   77

    9 Managing Difficult Conversations   84

    10 Digital Communication   94

    11 Building Relationships and Networks   104

Part III: Advanced Leadership Communication   111

    12 Negotiation and Persuasion   112

    13 Crisis Communication   119

14 Building and Sustaining a Culture of Effective Com   136

The Last Word   144

References   146

Further Reading   152

First Printing, 2025
Cover by Luke Hill
Edited by Jennifer Stone
Hardcover ISBN: 979-8-9927604-0-8
Paperback ISBN: 979-8-9927604-1-5
Printed in the United States
First Edition
Published by Hill & Henderson Solutions

Introduction

L eadership communication isn't just about talking; it's about orchestrating a symphony of understanding, influence, and inspiration. It's the conductor's baton that guides the orchestra (or an organization) towards its shared goals. While all communication involves the exchange of information, leadership communication transcends the mere conveyance of facts. It involves a strategic, empathetic, and purposeful approach to influencing and motivating others to achieve a collective vision. It's about connecting with individuals on an emotional level, understanding their perspectives, and building relationships that foster trust and collaboration.

Think of a seasoned CEO delivering a compelling vision for the future to a room full of investors. Their words aren't just data points; they paint a vivid picture, evoking confidence, excitement, and a shared belief in the company's potential. This is the transformative power of leadership communication in action. It's the ability to not only convey information but also inspire action, build consensus, and drive organizational change.

Unlike general communication, which may focus on the straightforward exchange of information, leadership communication requires a deeper level of awareness and skill. It demands a keen understanding of your audience, the ability to adapt your message to different contexts, and the skill to navigate complex interpersonal dynamics. It's about influencing behavior, shaping perceptions, and creating that shared sense of purpose that drives organizations forward. It's a skill, not an innate talent—meaning it can be developed anywhere by anyone. The lessons contained in these pages contain the keys to cultivate and master the art of leadership communication.

Effective leadership communication underpins every aspect of successful leadership. Consider a team leader struggling to motivate their team. Poor communication can lead to confusion, frustration, and decreased productivity. Conversely, a leader who effectively communicates expectations, provides constructive feedback, and fosters open dialogue creates an environment where team members are empowered and motivated to excel. This translates to team cohesion, increased motivation, and the achievement of organizational goals.

The impact of leadership communication extends far beyond the confines of a single team. It influences decision making processes, shaping the direction and strategy of an organization. Clear, concise, and well-articulated communication ensures that all stakeholders–from employees to board members to customers–are all aligned and working towards the same objectives. Consider the challenge of implementing significant organizational change. Without effective communication, resistance, confusion, and ultimately, failure, are likely. However, a leader who expertly communicates the rationale for change, manages concerns and fosters collaboration, will navigate the transition smoothly and successfully.

In these pages, we will explore the nuances of communicating to command, split into three sections. The first will outline the pillars of leadership communication, including understanding the virtues of leadership, the importance of understanding your audience, as well as the significance of active listening, and finally, non-verbal communication. In the second section, we will see leadership communication in action, which includes chapters on public speaking in a leadership role, inspiring and motivating others, along with coaching and mentoring, managing difficult conversations, and how to utilize digital communication effectively. We will end the section by delving into building relationships and networks. In the third and final section, we will discuss advanced leadership communication strategies for negotiation and persuasion, as well as the complexities of crisis communication.

It is worth noting that the lessons within this book are meant as a guide, not an end-all-be-all rulebook for leadership communication. Different situations demand different strategies. A highly assertive style might be appropriate when delivering critical feedback, while a more collaborative approach is essential when navigating disagreements within your team. A leader who can adapt their communication style to the context and the audience will be far more effective than a leader who relies on a singular, inflexible method.

This ability to adapt your communication to the nuances of various contexts is critical. Delivering a presentation to the board of directors requires a significantly different approach than addressing a team meeting. The formality, level of detail, and emphasis on data will vary greatly. Similarly, communicating with individual team members necessitates a personalized approach, considering individual strengths, weaknesses, and communication preferences. Ignoring these differences can result in misinterpretations, misunderstandings, and ultimately, failed communication.

Finally, it is worth noting that this book is meant for those working their way up to leadership positions, as well as those already there. You will read sentences that refer to leaders in the second person, as well as the third. The interchanging of referring to leaders as you, the reader (second person) as well as someone else (third person) was intentional, in order to not alienate anyone from the lessons included within.

We hope you gain valuable insights in your journey toward effective leadership communication.

Part I: Foundations of Leadership Communication

CHAPTER 1

The Heart of Leadership – Empathy

Your greatest skill isn't what you do. It's how you make others feel working with you.
-Andrea Petrone

In this world, there are two types of people that command others; bosses, and leaders. After reading that sentence, someone who you've worked for probably sprung to mind that falls distinctly into one of those categories.

These two types of people are usually separated by a single trait; *empathy*. Empathy is about actively understanding the emotional landscape of another individual. It's about stepping into their shoes, feeling what they feel, and understanding their perspective from within. This profound capacity is not merely an integral trait of a leader; it's the very foundation upon which impactful leadership is built. This is why we are starting with empathy; how can you expect to master leadership communication if you are not a leader first?

The neural pathways associated with empathy are intricately woven into our brain's architecture. Mirror neurons, for instance, fire both when we perform an action and when we observe someone else performing the same action. This mirroring effect contributes to our ability to understand and share the emotions and experiences of others [1].

Furthermore, the anterior insular cortex, a key player in emotional processing, plays a crucial role in our empathetic responses. When we witness another person's distress, our own anterior insular cortex becomes activated, triggering an emotional response that allows us to connect with their experience [2]. These natural processes support the powerful human capacity for understanding and sharing the feelings of others.

It is crucial to differentiate between sympathy and empathy. Sympathy represents a feeling of pity or sorrow for another's misfortune, often while maintaining a detached perspective. Empathy, on the other hand, involved a deeper, more immersive understanding. It's about genuinely feeling with the other person, sharing their emotional experience as if it were your own. This distinction is vital because while sympathy can be helpful, empathy is far more potent in building genuine connections and trust, two integral parts of being a leader.

Empathetic communication isn't simply about expressing words of comfort or understanding; it's about actively demonstrating that you have listened, understood, and have validated their feelings. Effective leaders showcase their emotional intelligence by engaging in active listening, validating emotions expressed by their team members, and responding appropriately to the diverse emotional expressions within their teams. This might involve acknowledging the validity of their feelings, even if you don't agree with their perspective. It might include asking open-ended questions to understand their experience better. It could even entail simply offering a quiet presence of support if they need it.

Consider a scenario where a team member is struggling with a personal challenge that is affecting their work performance. A *boss* will only focus on the impact of productivity, displaying a lack of empathy, and may even make it known that repercussions may be in order if the team member's performance does not improve. *Bosses* care only about performance, not the individual themselves. Because of this, a *boss* will not have the respect of their team members, and may struggle with a high employee turnover rate. In contrast, a *leader* would demonstrate genuine interest and concern; by validating the team member's feelings, and investing time in helping them overcome their struggle. This approach fosters trust, respect, and demonstrates that the leader cares about their team members beyond their work performance.

Building trust and mutual respect through empathetic communication is a cornerstone of effective collaboration. When team members feel understood and valued, they are more likely to be engaged, productive, and committed to achieving shared goals. They are more likely to openly share ideas, concerns, and challenges, creating a culture of open communication and collaboration. Conversely, a lack of empathy leads to a breakdown of trust and team conflict, creating an environment where team members feel unheard and undervalued. The cumulative effect is reduced morale and decreased productivity.

Empathetic communication extends beyond the immediate team; it's crucial in building strong relationships with clients, stakeholders, and even competitors. Understanding the needs, concerns, and perspectives of external parties is vital for creating strong partnerships, navigating challenging negotiations, and achieving mutually beneficial outcomes. It allows you to fully understand needs and preferences, ensuring satisfaction with your services. In interactions with stakeholders, empathy enables you to see the situation from multiple viewpoints and address concerns constructively, facilitating consensus and shared goals.

Think of a negotiation with a challenging client. A leader who approaches the negotiation with empathy will spend time listening to the client's concerns and understanding their needs. They will show genuine interest in finding a mutually beneficial solution, rather than just focusing on "winning" (you will learn more about this in chapter 12). This approach can result in a more robust and long-lasting relationship with the client.

In today's increasingly complex and interconnected world, understanding diverse perspectives is more essential than ever. The benefits of empathetic communication are far-reaching, influencing aspects like improved team morale, increased productivity, stronger client relationships, and ultimately, better overall organizational performance. The cultivation of empathy isn't *just* a soft skill; it's a fundamental leadership competency that directly impacts the bottom line. Therefore, actively fostering empathy through consistent practice and a genuine commitment to understanding others is a key investment in achieving sustainable success.

PRACTICAL STRATEGIES

Now that you understand the importance of empathetic communication, let's look at some practical strategies to hone this skill.

The first—and one that has its own chapter coming up and is interwoven throughout the lessons in these pages—is active listening. Active listening is a foundation of all communication. Active listening is not simply understanding the words that someone speaks, but truly understanding the complete message. This includes the verbal content, unspoken emotions, and the subtle nuances of body language. It's about receiving the message, processing it, and responding in a way that demonstrates genuine understanding and validation.

Another important technique is paraphrasing. This involves re-stating the speaker's message in your own words, ensuring you've correctly understood their meaning. For instance, if a team member expresses frustration about a project deadline, you might respond, "So, it sounds like you're feeling overwhelmed by the tight deadline and concerned about meeting all the requirements." Paraphrasing not only confirms your understanding but also shows the speaker that you truly *hear* them. It also provides an opportunity for clarification and ensures that you're both on the same page while demonstrating respect for the speaker's perspective and encourages them to elaborate, fostering deeper understanding. Poor paraphrasing indicates a lack of attention or genuine engagement on the listener's part. Therefore, it is essential to accurately summarize what you have heard to build trust and rapport.

An additional powerful tool is reflecting feelings. This goes beyond simply understanding the content of the message; it involves identifying and acknowledging the speaker's emotions. If a colleague is visibly upset about a missed opportunity, acknowledging their disappointment goes a long way in validating their feelings and creating a safe space for them to express themselves further. This technique further demonstrates empathy and strengthens the emotional connection between the listener and speaker.

It can also help de-escalate potentially tense situations. Imagine a scenario where a client expresses anger over a delayed product delivery. Simply reflecting the client's feelings—"I understand you're feeling frustrated and angry about the delay"--can drastically change a negative interaction by showing their emotions are being acknowledged and understood, which lays the groundwork for a more constructive conversation and a mutually acceptable solution.

However, the path to effective listening isn't without obstacles. Several common communication barriers can hinder our ability to truly understand others. Preconceived notions and biases can cloud our judgment, preventing us from seeing things from another person's perspective. Overcoming this requires conscious self-reflection and a commitment to setting aside personal prejudices. Active listening training can equip leaders with techniques for acknowledging their biases and focusing on factual information rather than misperceptions, fostering better objectivity and decision-making.

Interrupting or finishing people's sentences are another stumbling block to communication, as it conveys a lack of respect for the speaker, signaling the listener is more interested in their own thoughts than in understanding the other person's message. It cultivates an atmosphere where the speaker feels unheard and undervalued, leading to communication breakdown. This can be particularly damaging in negotiations of conflict-resolution situations, causing significant harm to trust and rapport. Practicing patience by allowing the speaker to fully express their thoughts without interruption is paramount. The active listener should focus entirely on the speaker's message, reserving their responses for appropriate moments and allowing for thoughtful consideration before speaking.

Similarly, filtering or selectively hearing information based on one's own interests or biases is a significant impediment to true empathetic listening. It leads to misinterpretations and prevents leaders from forming a complete picture of the situation or understanding the speaker's complete message. To combat this, active listeners must consciously avoid filtering and make an effort to understand the full context of the message, even if it includes unpleasant or inconvenient information.

Defensiveness is another obstacle that can significantly impede effective listening. When we feel attacked or criticized, our natural inclination is to become defensive, thereby hindering our ability to listen objectively and understand the other person's perspective which shuts down communication and prevents open dialogue. Leaders must consciously work to control their defensive reactions, focusing instead on understanding the speaker's point of view, even if it's critical. By acknowledging and validating the speaker's concerns, leaders can create a safe environment for open communication and reduce defensiveness.

Overcoming these barriers requires a conscious effort to develop self-awareness and refine listening skills. Practicing mindfulness can significantly enhance our ability to focus on the present moment and truly hear what others are saying. This involves setting aside our own thoughts and worries and focusing our full attention on the speaker. Meditation and mindfulness exercises can help train our minds to be more present and attentive, improving overall listening capacity. Leaders who cultivate mindfulness are better equipped to handle stressful situations, control their emotions, and engage in empathetic listening.

Mastering the art of empathy requires effort, self-reflection, and a commitment to ongoing learning. By actively practicing the techniques outlined in this section and continuing to refine your listening skills, you can significantly enhance your ability to build strong relationships, resolve conflicts effectively, and create a thriving and productive work environment where team members respect you. The true measure of empathetic leadership is the positive impact it has on both individual relationships and overall team success.

CHAPTER 2

Understanding Your Audience

There is a great difference between knowing and understanding: you can know a lot about something and not really understand it.
-Charles Kettering

Understanding your audience is essential for the success of any organization or individual. Whether engaging external stakeholders, clients, customers, or working with your internal team, knowing their unique needs and expectations allows you to tailor your messages, strategies, and approaches to resonate effectively. This leads to higher engagement, greater satisfaction, and increased impact.

Knowing your audience allows you to craft messages that directly address their concerns and interests. For instance, a business trying to increase sales must understand the motivations of different customer types. Internally, understanding your team involves recognizing their strengths, weaknesses, and preferences, leading to better collaboration and a more harmonious work environment.

A deep understanding of your audience benefits the entire organization, from leadership to staff. When leaders know their team members, they can delegate more effectively, boost morale, and foster a culture of respect and collaboration. Staff who feel understood are more likely to stay engaged, motivated, and committed to the organization's goals.

STEPS TO IDENTIFY YOUR AUDIENCE

To effectively engage your audience, you must identify who they are and what they need.

Begin by defining your goals

Articulating what you aim to achieve helps ensure all team members are aligned and working towards the same objectives. Ask yourself if your goal is to; increase sales, improve customer engagement, or boost team productivity, knowing your goals helps you identify the right audience to target.

Understand *their* challenges

When identifying your audience, you must act empathetically and demonstrate that you understand their unique challenges and motivations. This involves more than relying on subjective opinions; it requires gathering concrete evidence. Research suggests that understanding your audience profoundly and acting empathetically can lead to more effective communication and stronger relationships. For example, a study published in the Journal of Experimental Social Psychology in 2020 found that attending live theater can significantly increase empathy and prosocial behavior, suggesting that immersing yourself in your audience's experiences can lead to a deeper understanding and more effective communication [3].

Research

Conduct research to gather data about your audience through surveys, interviews, and available demographic insights. Utilize tools like Google Analytics, social media insights, and customer surveys to collect quantitative data (e.g., age, income level) and qualitative data (e.g., interests, values, challenges). These methods provide a more objective and reliable understanding of your audience than subjective, opinion-based approaches.

Create audience personas

This can be done by developing detailed profiles that represent your typical audience members. These personas should include demographic information like age, gender, occupation, and psychographic details like interests, challenges, and personal goals. Humanizing your audience helps you better understand their specific needs and preferences.

Segment your audience into smaller, more manageable groups based on shared traits. This segmentation will allow you to craft personalized messages and strategies tailored to each group.

Listen and engage

Truly hearing what your audience has to say and engaging with them using direct communication channels such as surveys, feedback forms, and social media interactions. Building relationships through these touchpoints will deepen your understanding of their needs.

TAILORING YOUR MESSAGE

Now that you've gathered insights about your audience, it's time to craft your message. Tailoring it for maximum impact requires a few strategic approaches:

Use audience-centric language by speaking the language of your audience. Avoid jargon or industry-specific terms that might confuse them. Use clear, accessible language that connects with their experiences. Adjust your speech, as everyone doesn't think and understand things similarly. As discussed in the previous section, this can be achieved by asking questions and getting background information on your audience.

Highlight benefits by focusing on what your audience will receive from your offerings. Whether it's a product, service, or idea, demonstrate how your solution addresses their needs and provides value. It's important to give your audience a view into the future by properly explaining the value of what you are discussing. This can help people focus and become interested. Share stories that engage people on an emotional level. Share narratives that illustrate the impact of your work and how it has helped others. Storytelling makes your message more relatable and memorable.

Be authentic. Authenticity builds trust. Be honest in your communications, showing that you genuinely care about your audience's needs. When your audience believes in the sincerity of your message, they are more likely to engage. The level of influence someone authentic can build is significant; it can be an excellent opportunity to encourage people to listen to you and trust you.

INTERNAL PERSPECTIVE: UNDERSTANDING YOUR TEAM

Audience understanding isn't limited to external stakeholders—it's equally vital to understand your internal audience—your team. When internal teams understand one another's strengths, weaknesses, and working styles, it leads to smoother collaboration and a more effective organization. There are a few effective ways to do this;

Direct engagement

Engaging your internal audience directly impacts your ability to engage external stakeholders effectively. Regularly check in with your team members through one-on-one meetings, surveys, or informal conversations to stay informed about their needs and challenges.

Open communication

Foster open communication by creating a culture where team members feel comfortable expressing their thoughts, feedback, and ideas. Open communication fosters trust and ensures alignment across the organization.

Build inter-team knowledge

Encourage team members to learn about one another's roles and working styles to promote team understanding. Facilitating this understanding can improve collaboration and help everyone work toward shared goals.

Consistent training and development

Offer regular training and development opportunities. This helps individual team members grow and strengthens the organization's overall capabilities.

PRACTICAL EXAMPLES FOR UNDERSTANDING YOUR TEAM

Implementing strategies to understand your team can lead to a more cohesive and effective organization. One effective method is conducting regular check-ins. These one-on-one meetings help leaders stay informed about team members' progress, challenges, and goals, providing timely support and fostering open communication.

Anonymous surveys are another valuable tool for gathering insights on team satisfaction, challenges, and suggestions for improvement. These surveys encourage honest feedback, which can be critical for making informed decisions about changes needed to enhance team dynamics. Research by The Society for Human Resource Management (SHRM) highlights that regular employee feedback is linked to higher job satisfaction and performance [4].

Team-building activities are also essential for improving communication and strengthening relationships among team members. These activities range from casual social gatherings to structured workshops to build trust and collaboration.

Cross-training programs are another great way for team members to better understand the inner workings of the organization. A cross-training program is where team members learn about a role or task they don't typically perform within the organization. By having team members do this, they will broaden skill sets, promote empathy, and encourage a sense of shared responsibility among team members. By understanding each other's roles and responsibilities, team members can better appreciate their colleagues' contributions and work more effectively together.

Collaborative projects offer opportunities for team members to work together towards common goals, helping individuals appreciate each other's strengths and contributions. These projects can promote a more cohesive team environment and improve overall performance.

Studies supporting these strategies show that effective team understanding and collaboration can significantly impact organizational success. For example, a meta-analysis published in Frontiers of Psychology found that team-building activities were positively associated with team performance, highlighting the importance of encouraging team cohesion [5].

MONITORING AND ADAPTING YOUR STRATEGY

Audience understanding is an ongoing process, and practical strategies must be adaptable. As your audience's needs, preferences, and behaviors evolve, so should your approach. Consistently tracking and analyzing data ensures you remain aligned with your audience's expectations, helping you stay relevant and practical.

Use analytics tools to monitor audience behavior. Digital tools like website metrics, email engagement data, and social media insights offer valuable information about your audience.

Gather feedback regularly through quick polls, post-event surveys, and direct communications to keep your finger on the pulse. Periodically assess the feedback and data you collect to identify emerging trends and patterns. For instance, if a segment of your audience engages more with specific types of content or messaging, analyze what elements contribute to this success and consider applying them across other segments.

Adjust strategies based on insights. Refine your messaging, communication channels, and content types to better meet your audience's needs. Stay informed about industry changes to anticipate shifts in audience behavior and expectations.

AUDIENCE PERSONAS ACROSS INDUSTRIES

Understanding your audience is not a one-size-fits-all process. Different industries offer valuable insights for developing more relatable and impactful audience personas. By looking at how other sectors approach their audiences, you can identify trends and strategies that apply to your organization, even if your mission differs.

For example, a company focused on supporting families might learn from how healthcare organizations design programs for individuals facing chronic health issues. Similarly, a business that relies on customer loyalty could find valuable insights by studying how successful brands engage loyal customers, emphasizing relationship-building and personalization.

Organizations can craft more dynamic and audience-focused engagement strategies by borrowing strategies and insights from industries like retail, technology, and healthcare. The goal is not to copy but to adapt effective practices to your organization's needs. Industries often deal with similar audience dynamics—people have needs, preferences, and concerns that can be addressed in ways that transcend industry boundaries.

GATHERING AUDIENCE FEEDBACK EFFECTIVELY

Collecting direct feedback from your audience is vital to truly understanding your audience and refining your messaging. This feedback serves as the foundation for more targeted, relevant communication. Various methods can be employed to gather this feedback, each offering advantages depending on your needs.

Surveys and questionnaires allow you to ask specific questions that yield both quantitative and qualitative data. Online survey platforms provide easy-to-use tools to create customized surveys and analyze responses, helping you capture a wide range of audience opinions. To maximize the effectiveness of surveys, ensure questions are clear and relevant and offer an incentive for completion to increase response rates.

Offering incentives for participation is a proven method to encourage higher response rates. Incentives can include discounts, entries into a prize draw, or exclusive content. These rewards can motivate your audience to share their honest opinions, providing you with valuable insights.

Conducting in-depth interviews with a diverse sample of your audience allows for comprehensive insights. Use open-ended questions to encourage detailed responses. These interviews provide a deeper understanding of your audience's thoughts and feelings, which can be invaluable for tailoring your communication strategies.

Hosting focus groups can facilitate discussions on specific topics, providing a comfortable setting where participants feel safe to share their honest opinions. This method allows for interactive dialogue and can reveal collective viewpoints and emerging trends.

Utilizing social media listening tools helps monitor online conversations and gauge sentiment. These tools track trends, keywords, and feedback across platforms, providing real-time information that might not be captured in formal surveys or interviews. By understanding ongoing conversations and sentiments about your brand or topics of interest, you can better adapt your messaging to meet your audience's needs.

Analyzing behavioral data with tools like Google Analytics allows you to track how your audience interacts with your digital content. Look for patterns and trends that can inform your communication strategy. This data provides objective insights into what resonates with your audience, helping you refine your approach.

Regularly reviewing and adapting your strategies based on the data collected ensures you remain aligned with your audience's evolving needs and preferences. This ongoing process of feedback and adaptation is crucial for maintaining relevance and effectiveness in your communication efforts.

Implementing these practical steps can help you gain a deeper understanding of your audience, refine your messaging, and foster stronger connections.

CONTINUOUS LEARNING AND GROWTH

Always seek to learn and grow from your experiences. Embrace feedback, both positive and negative, as opportunities for improvement. Additionally, learning from the experiences and wisdom of others can greatly enhance your leadership skills. By understanding others' successes and failures, you can gain valuable insights that help you avoid common pitfalls and focus on improving weak areas of your approach.

Incorporating continuous learning into your routine can be as simple as reading industry-relevant books, attending workshops, and networking with peers. Staying informed about trends and best practices ensures you remain adaptable and effective in your communication strategies.

In essence, by deeply understanding and thoughtfully engaging with your audience, you command the ability to influence, inspire, and achieve your goals. This approach fosters loyalty and trust and paves the way for long-term success and growth in any endeavor.

CHAPTER 3

Active Listening

Most people do not listen with the intent to understand;
they listen with the intent to reply.
-Stephen Covey

Active listening is a cornerstone of effective communication, especially in leadership roles. It is much more than simply hearing what the speaker has to say, but actively engaging with their message and understanding their perspective. The ability to listen proactively unlocks profound benefits, which leads to deeper understanding, creating an environment for resolving conflicts, and building stronger relationships.

Imagine a scenario where you are leading a team working on a critical project. You're presented with a proposal from a team member, and initially, have a different perspective. Instead of immediately dismissing their idea or offering a counter-proposal, you can choose to listen actively. You attentively focus on your colleague's words, observing their body language, and asking clarifying questions to ensure you have gotten the full idea. You might ask questions like "So are you suggesting we approach this challenge from a different angle, and what specific benefits do you see in this approach?" Or, "I don't quite fully understand this idea, can you clarify what you mean?"

By actively listening, you not only gain a deeper understanding of the proposed solution, but also demonstrate a genuine interest and respect for your colleague's contributions.

The act of active listening can be transformative. It can bridge communication gaps, create a sense of value for the team member, and lead to more productive collaboration. Your active listening may uncover things you hadn't previously considered, leading to a more innovative and effective solution that incorporates both your initial perspective and your colleague's proposal.

Beyond the immediate benefits of understanding and collaboration, active listening plays a vital role in building trust and rapport. When people feel truly heard and understood, they are more likely to trust your judgment and respect your leadership. This trust is essential for effective communication, creating a safe and open environment where team members feel comfortable sharing their thoughts and concerns without fear of judgment.

As a leader, this type of culture of active listening is *critical* to instill in an organization, as making sure that employees feel seen and heard in the workplace gives everyone a sense of belonging, and encourages a culture of creativity and hard work ethic. It can also have added benefits like a decreased employee turnover rate. According to a study by Perceptyx, employers that regularly listen to employee feedback are **eleven** times more likely to have high employee retention levels, and three times as likely to hit financial targets [6].

Consider a scenario where a team member is facing a personal challenge that is impacting their work. They may hesitate to bring it up for fear of being perceived as weak or unprofessional. However, by creating a culture of active listening, you can encourage them to share their concerns, and feel safe in doing so. You might begin by asking "I've noticed you seem a bit preoccupied lately, is there anything you would like to talk about?" This simple gesture can open the door for their communication, allowing the team member to feel supported and understood. Your active listening might even lead to a solution that helps them overcome the challenge, ultimately benefiting both the individual and the team's overall performance.

Active listening also plays a crucial role in resolving conflicts. When disagreements arise, it is all too easy to become defensive, focusing on proving your point rather than truly understanding the person's perspective. However, active listening is the key to transforming these confrontations into constructive dialogues. By listening to the other party's perspective, and fully grasping their ideas, you can identify the root causes of the conflict and work towards a mutually acceptable solution.

Now imagine another scenario where two team members are locked in a heated debate over a project deadline. Both feel strongly about their position and are unwilling to compromise. If you, as the leader, jump in and try to impose a solution over them, you risk escalating the conflict and alienating both parties. This leaves both individuals frustrated and unmotivated. Instead, practicing active listening allows you to understand the concerns driving each perspective. You might ask "I hear you're concerned about the feasibility of meeting this deadline, can you elaborate your concerns?" Then, turn to the other team member saying, "I understand you're advocating for this deadline because of the importance of meeting our client's expectations. What are your thoughts on (the other party's) concerns?" By using this approach, you create an environment where both team members feel heard and understood, paving the way for finding a solution that addresses their concerns and avoids further conflict.

THE BARRIERS TO ACTIVE LISTENING

Now that we have looked at not only the benefits, but examples of active listening in the workplace, we must now confront the barriers that often stand in the way of active listening. These barriers can be subtle or overt, but they all have the potential to hinder our understanding and impact the quality of our interactions with one another.

Distractions

Ever present in our fast-paced world, from the pinging of notifications on our phones to the chatter of colleagues in the next cubicle, our attention is continually pushed and pulled in all directions. These distractions, however small they may seem in print, can chip away at your ability to truly listen and engage in meaningful dialogue.

Assumptions

These are mental shortcuts we take to make sense of the world around us. However, these shortcuts can also lead us down a path of misinterpretations and misunderstandings. In a conversation, assumptions can act like a filter, obscuring the true meaning of the message being conveyed. For instance, if a colleague is late to a meeting, we might automatically assume that this employee is disrespectful, disorganized, or maybe flat out doesn't care. However, there might be a completely valid reason, like a complete road closure, or sudden family emergency. It is always best to get the full story and not make assumptions.

In order to combat our assumptions, we need to shift our perspective. By consciously questioning our assumptions, challenging our biases, and seeking clarification when necessary, we can cultivate a more open and receptive approach to listening.

Emotions

Powerful drivers of our behavior, emotions can significantly impact our ability to listen effectively. If a colleague is expressing an opinion we disagree with, our frustrations might overshadow their words and message. In these instances, our emotions can become a barrier preventing us from truly hearing what they are saying, and their reasoning behind why they believe it.

Recognizing our own emotional triggers, taking a moment to calm yourself before responding, and actively listening to the other person's perspective without judgment are crucial steps in overcoming this barrier.

BREAKING DOWN THE BARRIERS

Overcoming these barriers to active listening is an ongoing journey that requires a conscious and consistent effort. Here are five key strategies to integrate into your daily interactions:

1. Cultivate Mindfulness

By being present in the moment and focusing your attention on the speaker, you can reduce the impact of distractions and create a space for deep listening.

2. Active Listening Techniques

By implementing active listening techniques like paraphrasing, summarizing, and asking clarifying questions, you demonstrate your engagement and ensure that you are understanding the message correctly.

3. Non-Verbal Communication

Pay attention to non-verbal cues such as body language, facial expressions, and tone of voice (this will be looked at more closely in the following chapter). These cues can provide valuable insights into the speaker's emotions and intentions.

4. Empathy and Emotional Intelligence

By developing your empathy and emotional intelligence, you gain the ability to understand and acknowledge the feelings and perspectives of others.

5. Feedback and Self-Reflection

Regularly seeking feedback from others on your listening skills is a great way to gain insight into your communication skills. This self-awareness can help you identify areas for improvement and refine your listening approach.

Active listening is much more than just a tool for communication, it's a mindset. It requires a willingness to set aside one's opinions and biases, truly listen to the other person's perspective, and above all, to demonstrate compassion and empathy. It is a skill that takes time to practice and develop, but the rewards are immeasurable. Active listening can transform your leadership style, build stronger relationships, and create a more productive and harmonious work environment. By embracing this fundamental principle of communication, you can elevate your leadership to new heights, creating greater understanding, better collaboration, and overall success.

CHAPTER 4

Nonverbal Communication

Nonverbal communication forms a social language that is in many ways richer and more fundamental than our words.
-Leonard Mlodinow

The world of communication is a vast and complex landscape, and nonverbal communication—the silent language of our bodies—plays a pivotal role in how we are perceived and understood. It's the subtle cues, the unspoken gestures, and the nuances of our physical presence that often speak louder than words. It is not about what you say, but what you don't, that can reveal your inner feelings to others. To truly master the art of leadership communication, we must first examine the powerful world of body language.

Imagine yourself in a meeting, presenting a key proposal. You have spent countless hours rehearsing every word, focusing merely on memorization. Each slide in the deck has been meticulously crafted, and finally, you get to show it off to your colleagues. Yet, as you get further and further into pitch, a subtle unease creeps in. You look around the room and notice your colleagues' eyes. Though fixed on the screen, they seem distant, uninterested, *bored.*

Is it the slides? The ideas? You spent all your time crafting this pitch, and you know the ideas are compelling, the data sound. What is missing?

The answer is your body language.

Your posture is rigid, arms crossed defensively, eyes darting nervously around the room. *You lost your audience before you even made it past the title slide.*

In order to captivate an audience, as we saw in this scenario, you need more than a great slide deck and solid ideas. You need to lose the rigidness in your shoulders, *relax,* and infuse your words with energy and passion. Gestures, confident eye contact, pausing every once in a while to let your carefully crafted words sink in for effect. These are all powerful examples that can dramatically change how you and your words are perceived.

Now let's imagine another scenario in which you are a recruiter choosing between two candidates. The first candidate puttered in with slumped shoulders as he stared at the floor. His handshake was limp, and, despite his qualifications, seemed to lack ambition and confidence throughout the entirety of the interview. Through his answers you can tell he is intelligent and mentally fit for the role. But this is not the candidate you want.

The next candidate strides in with an entirely different energy. Her handshake is firm, her smile warm, and her eye contact strong. She sits down, back straight, and answers each question with her voice enthusiastic and her eyes engaged in the interview. For the entirety of the conversation, her body language stayed consistent, showing her desire and zeal for the role.

Reflecting on the two interviews, you have a clear choice for who should get the role, despite both candidates having near identical qualifications. *Why?* Because communication is far more than just the words we speak. It is *how* we speak them. Our gaze, posture, and warmth speak louder than words. The critical truth is that words convey information, but your body language conveys your attitude and potential. This is why body language is one of the foundations of leadership communication. While leaders at all levels all over the world have different ways of speaking, their body language is universal. And in the following pages you will learn how to use your body language to your advantage.

THE ROLE OF BODY LANGUAGE

Body language encompasses a wide range of nonverbal cues, each carrying a unique message. These cues are often subconscious, emanating from our inner state and reflecting our emotions, intentions, and levels of confidence. It's the way we stand, the expressions on our faces, the movement of our hands, and the intensity of our gaze.

Studies have shown that first impressions of someone can be formed in as little as a single millisecond [7]. We have all heard the phrase "don't judge a book by its cover." But we as human beings do. It's a hard pill to swallow, but people are judgemental and it is difficult for them to change their perception once it has formed. As a leader, you need to be prepared to not only nail the first impression- but all subsequent moments from then on. Everything from posture to clothing to your handshake and eye contact all matter and create the perception of yourself in the other person's mind.

That is exactly *why* it is imperative to always leave a great first impression. In these initial moments of meeting someone, our body language becomes a silent ambassador, conveying volumes about our character, professionalism, and even our level of preparedness, without even saying a single word.

In 1971, Dr. Albert Mehrabain, a UCLA psychology professor broke down the components of face to face communication in his book *Silent Messages*. He states that communication is only 7% of the words spoken, 38% tonality, and 55% nonverbal [8].

The breakthrough of this book was the finding that less than a tenth of communication is in the actual words coming out of our mouths. The tone and even more so the nonverbal communication, is the largest part of communicating with others. With this in mind, let's take a look at how you can master that 55% and communicate like a leader should, by taking a look at the following strategies;

Posture

A cornerstone of powerful body language, posture is the way we hold ourselves, the alignment of our body, and the subtle shifts in our stance. A confident posture exudes an aura of authority and composure, signaling to others that you are engaged, attentive, and ready to lead.

But the effects of good posture are not relegated to changing how others perceive you. Good posture also helps facilitate good respiration and strong voice projection.

Think of a speaker standing tall, shoulders relaxed, back straight, and an ever so subtle upward tilt of the head. This posture communicates confidence, attentiveness, and an openness to engaging with the audience. In contrast, slouching, crossed arms, and a downward gaze convey a sense of disinterest, insecurity, and even hostility.

Facial Expressions

Our faces hold such power in the way they can communicate without ever saying a word. Think of some of the greatest actors of our time-from DeNiro to Denzel. The emotions they can convey in scenes, without speaking, is immensely powerful. Frustration, longing, and sorrow-can all be achieved with the eyes alone. While you don't need to have an Academy Award sitting at home to convey feelings and emotions through facial expressions, you can learn to leverage it to your advantage.

A warm smile can build rapport, a furrowed brow can signal concern, and a raised eyebrow can convey skepticism. These expressions are involuntary responses to our inner state, but we can consciously manage them to create the desired impression.

Now think of a CEO delivering a speech to employees. A genuine smile, coupled with a reassuring nod, inspires confidence and trust. However, a tense jaw, an unblinking gaze, and a forced smile can come across as insincere and create a barrier to connection.

Eye Contact

Perfecting eye contact is a powerful tool for engaging with others. It conveys attentiveness, respect, and sincerity. Direct eye contact, without being overly intense, shows that you are present, listening, and genuinely interested in what the other person has to say.

Eye contact can be used for much more than engaging with others. A popular study from the Idiap Research Institute found that eye contact can be an indicator of social hierarchy and dominance in a conversation. This institute found that leaders not only look at the person speaking for a longer period, but also receive more eye contact in return [9]. Another study that analyzed the eye contact of 3,000 people found that during conversation, the average person will make eye contact between 30-60% of the time, but in order to establish an emotional connection with someone that number should be between 60-70% [10].

Now consider a manager conducting a performance review with an employee. Maintaining consistent eye contact throughout the conversation, while listening intently to the employee's feedback, shows respect, attentiveness, and genuine interest in them as a human being, not just an employee. Holding eye contact for longer shows dominance in the conversation, and lets the employee know who is in control of the conversation.

Gestures

These are the subtle movements of our hands and arms, which can be used to reinforce our verbal communication or add emphasis to our message. Open gestures, like extended palms, or expansive hand movements, signal openness, confidence, and a willingness to engage. Closed gestures, like crossed arms or clenched fists, show defensiveness, insecurity, or a lack of engagement.

For decades studies have shown the effectiveness of using gestures when speaking. A study conducted in 2024 sought to find the average number of hand gestures used in the most and least viewed TED talks online. This study found that the least viewed videos-that is, the ones that failed to captivate the viewer-used an average of 272 hand gestures (or 15 per minute). While this may seem like a high number, the most viewed TED talks in this study had an average of 465 hand gestures (almost 26 per minute) [11].

Another study conducted by psychologist Markus Koppensteiner attempted to find the ways in which our personalities are perceived by others–on our hand gestures alone. Koppensteiner took videos of political speeches, and animated them with stick figures and took away the audio, so that any personal bias or political views would not taint the results. Participants were then asked what personality traits they thought of when viewing the animated figures. While some traits, like conscientiousness, were difficult to gauge based on the gestures alone, others were much more apparent. For example, participants thought of the animated figures that used frequent, dynamic hand movements to be more extroverted. Perceptions of authority on the other hand, were linked to vertical movement. Politicians who made sweeping gestures from the lectern to shoulder height were often rated as more dominant, but also less agreeable [12].

In a 2015 paper, Koppensteiner argued that these personality ratings could accurately predict audience response in the real world videos these animated silent videos were based on. Not only could these ratings forecast applause levels, but they could also predict if the politician might face heckling. This suggests that while dominant gestures may command attention and respect, they can also be viewed as aggressive or arrogant if these types of gestures are over or misused [13].

Congruence

An often overlooked aspect of nonverbal communication is congruence. Our body language is most effective when it is in tune with our verbal communication. If our words say one thing, but our body language suggests something else, the message becomes confused and contradictory.

For example, if a leader expresses enthusiasm for a new project but their facial expressions and body language remain passive, the audience will likely perceive a lack of genuine interest. To maximize the impact of communication, it is crucial to ensure that our verbal and nonverbal cues are aligned properly.

By paying close attention to your posture, facial expressions, eye contact, gestures, and the congruence between your words and body language, you can take advantage of nonverbal communication as a leader.

Reading Nonverbal cues

Now that we have explored how to use *our own* non verbal communication to our advantage, lets now turn our attention to *other people's*.

It is first important to note that you will meet people that have a wide range of personality types, and their nonverbal cues may naturally differ from others. Consider for example, an introverted individual. An introvert might naturally exhibit less expressive body language than an extrovert, not because they are less engaged in the conversation, but simply because their personality is less outwardly demonstrative. A leader who interprets their subdued demeanor as disinterest or lack of engagement could miss opportunities for meaningful connection and mentorship. Understanding an individual's baseline behavior is imperative before drawing conclusions based on nonverbal cues.

Situational context is arguably equally as important. A person avoiding eye contact more than usual is normally a cause for concern. But if the individual is exhibiting this behavior during a performance review, it could very likely be due to the high-stress nature of the situation (especially if there is no cause for concern regarding performance).

Further, the environment itself can significantly shape nonverbal communication. A brightly lit, open office might encourage more relaxed and open body language, while a dimly lit, cramped room could very well lead to more reserved and guarded behavior. Noise levels, temperature, and even the seating arrangement can all influence how individuals present themselves nonverbally. As a leader, you can't simply have a cheat sheet of nonverbal cues to look out for and what they mean, as various factors influence this behavior. The best leaders read the situation and adapt their interpretation accordingly.

Developing your capacity to accurately interpret nonverbal cues goes hand-in-hand with cultivating strong intuition and emotional intelligence. While keen observation is crucial for picking up on subtle shifts in body language, facial expressions, and tone of voice, it's your intuitive understanding and emotional awareness that provide the context and depth necessary for truly effective interpretation. Without these elements, you may see the signals, but you might miss the meaning entirely. Intuition, often described as a "gut" feeling or a flash of insight, is not simply guesswork (though it is commonly mistaken for such); it's the culmination of your subconscious processing vast amounts of information gathered over time. This accumulated knowledge, coupled with your emotional intelligence, allows for you to connect the nonverbal cues to the underlying emotions and motivations driving the behavior.

Consider this scenario: You're leading a meeting pitching a new project, and a team member, while verbally agreeing to a new project, subtly avoids eye contact, fidgets with their pen, and their shoulders remain slumped throughout the duration of the meeting. A purely observational approach might note these nonverbal cues, but without emotional intelligence and intuition, you might simply label them as signs of nervousness and move on. However, a leader with well-developed intuition and emotional intelligence would delve deeper. They might consider the individual's past performance, their workload, and their overall disposition, and recognize that the nonverbal cues aren't just about nervousness, but instead may indicate a feeling of being overwhelmed, lacking confidence in their ability to succeed, or even silently resisting the project.

This more intuitive response allows for a more empathetic conversation, addressing the underlying concerns and providing the support needed to instill confidence and successful project completion.

Improving your own emotional intelligence is a critical component of enhancing your ability to interpret nonverbal communication of others. It involves self-awareness, self-regulation, social awareness, and relationship management. These four pillars are interconnected and are mutually reinforcing in the context of reading nonverbal cues.

Self-awareness allows for you to recognize your own biases and emotional responses, ensuring that they don't cloud your judgment when interpreting others' nonverbal behavior.

Self-regulation involves managing your own emotions so that you can approach interactions with others with a sense of clarity and objectivity.

Social awareness is the ability to emphasize with others, to understand their perspectives and emotions. This is fundamental in interpreting nonverbal cues accurately, as it allows you to consider the context of the situation and the individual's personal circumstances.

Finally, relationship management encompasses your ability to build and maintain healthy relationships. By skillfully navigating social interactions, you create an environment where individuals feel comfortable expressing themselves both verbally and nonverbally, leading to better communication.

With these lessons out of the way, let's now look at some nonverbal cues and their (likely) meanings:

Body Posture and Orientation

A person's posture–whether they are slumped or upright–speaks volumes about the individual's confidence and mood. Similarly, their orientation toward or away from you indicates their level of engagement and interest. A direct orientation for instance indicates full engagement. Similarly, leaning slightly forward or even mirroring another person's posture are another proven way to signify this [14].

On the other hand, leaning back suggests disengagement and disinterest, and turning away entirely signifies a desire to end the interaction. In group settings, orientation reveals alliances and power dynamics. An upright, expansive posture projects dominance, with shoulders back, chest out, and a raised head visually claiming authority and leading to a perception of leadership [15]. On the other end of the spectrum is a slumped, contracted posture, which signals submission and lack of confidence. These postural cues amplify or mitigate perceptions of power and authority.

In group interactions, orientation reveals alliances and hierarchy. For example, those who are closely aligned, with their bodies angled towards each other, demonstrate either a shared interest or pre-existing bond. Individuals who turn away or create physical distance, may be indicating disagreement, disinterest, or even a desire to distance themselves from the prevailing group dynamic.

Hand Gestures and Movements

Hands are remarkably expressive tools, revealing emotions often hidden by words. Fidgeting or excessive hand movements, such as tapping fingers or wringing hands, signals nervousness, anxiety, or discomfort, indicating unease or a lack of composure [16]. However, context is crucial, as some fidgeting is to be expected in high-pressure situations.

Open palms can convey honesty and sincerity, while clasped hands can sometimes signal defensiveness or anxiety [17]. Other gestures that involve touching one's face, can indicate nervousness or even deception (though this can also signal that someone is in deep thought).

Pupil Dilation

A subconscious response to interest or excitement, dilated pupils can signal engagement or attraction [18]. Conversely, constricted pupils might indicate discomfort, disapproval, or lack of interest. However, it is important to remember that lighting conditions always affect pupil size, and this may not be a consistent gauge.

Changes in Blinking Rate

An increase in blinking rate can suggest stress, anxiety, or deception [19]. A decrease can indicate focus or concentration.

Changes in Breathing

Rapid or shallow breathing has been linked to stress or anxiety, while slow deep breaths suggest calmness and composure [20].

It's critical to emphasize that interpreting nonverbal cues requires more than simply recognizing individual signals. It's the *combination* of cues that provides the most accurate interpretation. For instance, observing a person's slightly dilated pupils, a rapid blinking rate, and a slight slump in their posture might collectively suggest a high level of stress or anxiety, even if these cues are not overtly obvious in isolation.

Practicing your skills in recognizing these cues requires effort. Start by paying closer attention to the nonverbal communication of the people around you. Watch news broadcasts, observe people in casual settings, and consciously look for subtle shifts in their expressions and body language. This regular practice, coupled with thoughtful observation and critical analysis, is key to developing this skill. By refining your skill set it can provide profound advantages towards becoming a more effective leader.

Part II: Leadership Communication in Action

CHAPTER 5

The Role of Public Speaking in Leadership

The worst speech you'll ever give, will be far better than the one you never give.
-Fred Miller

The silence before a presentation. The glare of the stage lights. The expectant faces in the audience are a sea of potential judgment. For many, the prospect of public speaking triggers a cascade of physiological responses: a racing heart, pounding within your chest, sweaty palms, slowly corroding the edges of the notes they hold, that familiar knot tightening in your stomach that can only be relieved by leaving the stage. This is stage fright, a shared experience, even among seasoned professionals. It is also one of the most prevalent fears in the world, affecting a staggering 77% of people [14].

But stage fright doesn't have to be a crippling barrier. It can be managed, understood, and even harnessed to enhance performance.

Let's start by acknowledging that nervousness is natural. It's your body's way of preparing you for a challenge. Think of it as a surge of adrenaline, that extra energy that can be channeled into a powerful and engaging presentation. You may be wondering, then, why nervousness can be debilitating. That happens when your body overdoes this feeling; instead of being a motivator, it becomes paralyzing.

Reframing your perception of this nervousness is the key to overcoming stage fright. Instead of seeing it as a threat to your performance up on the stage, as many people do, view it as a sign that you're ready to perform, that you care deeply about your message, and that you're invested in its success.

One of the most effective strategies for combating stage fright is thorough preparation. This isn't about memorizing your script; it's about deeply understanding your material. This is so that if you lose your place in your memorized speech, you can improvise and still stay on track. This is also an old theatre trick: by understanding your character and the material you are working with, if you find yourself forgetting a line, you can adlib and make it work within the context of the scene and the storyline. You also learn in theatre that if you adlib, you must always veer the scene back on track as soon as possible. Ad-libbing will bridge the gap between your lapse in memory and get you back on track to the next part of your script that you remember.

It's also important to note that the more familiar you are with your content, the more confident you will feel. This preparation should also extend beyond the content itself. Consider the physical space where you'll be presenting. Visit the location beforehand (if possible) to familiarize yourself with the setup, including the lighting and layout, as well as the overall atmosphere. This reduces the element of surprise.

Regarding public speaking, the importance of practice cannot be understated. Don't just run through your presentation once or twice; rehearse it as often as you need until you know the material from front to back. It helps rehearse before a trusted friend, colleague, or mentor. This allows for valuable feedback and enables you to identify areas for improvement, both in content and delivery. Consider recording yourself to analyze your body language, tone, and pacing. Watching yourself on video can provide invaluable insights into areas you might not otherwise notice.

Visualization is another powerful tool. Before your presentation, take some time to rehearse your delivery mentally. Imagine confidently walking onto the stage, engaging with the audience, and delivering your message with clarity and passion. Focus on positive feelings of accomplishment and success. This mental rehearsal can significantly reduce anxiety and increase your sense of self-assurance. A study conducted in 2023 by Frontiers In Human Neuroscience found that practicing body awareness, simulation, visualization techniques, and gesture enhancement reduced self-reported measures of anxiety in participants by 33.2% [15]

On the day of your presentation, remember to take care of yourself physically. Get enough sleep, eat a balanced meal, and stay hydrated. Avoid both alcohol and caffeine (if possible), as these can drive up anxiety. Engage in relaxation techniques, such as deep breathing exercises or meditation, to calm your nerves and center yourself before you take the stage.

KEY STRATEGIES FOR PUBLIC SPEAKING

In addition to thorough preparation, there are a few key strategies to ace your presentation;

Understand Your Audience

Consider the audience's background and experience when creating your presentation. Are they experts, novices, or somewhere in between? Suppose you're speaking to a group of cybersecurity professionals about a new software platform. In that case, your technical jargon should be different than if you were presenting to a group of small business owners. You can dive into technical details for cybersecurity professionals, emphasizing the software's capabilities and integration nuances. Small business owners should focus on the practical benefits and demonstrate how the software will streamline operations and increase efficiency. Avoid overwhelming either group with information irrelevant to their existing knowledge base. Remember, your goal is clarity and engagement, not to showcase your expertise through obscure terminology.

Engage your audience early

A common mistake is to begin a presentation detached and formally. Instead, aim to connect with your audience from the very start. A warm smile, a brief anecdote, or a relevant question can instantly create a rapport and put people at ease, including yourself. Remember that audiences are rooting for you to succeed; they want your presentation to be informative and engaging.

Remember the power of storytelling

Humans are inherently drawn to narratives. We have been telling tales around campfires for millennia. A well-crafted story resonates with your audience, cutting through the noise of daily life and connecting with listeners on a visceral level. Think about your favorite TED Talk. What made it memorable? Chances are, it wasn't just the data points but the compelling narrative woven around those facts. It was a journey, a transformation, or a struggle that was overcome.

So, how do you weave compelling narratives into your presentations? First, identify the core message you want to convey. What's the central theme, the overarching idea that will resonate with your audience? Then, structure your presentation around a narrative arc. This classic storytelling structure involves a clear beginning, rising action, climax, falling action, and resolution. Consider the hero's journey–a standard narrative structure that resonates with the masses. Your presentation can follow a similar pattern, with your message as the central goal, challenges encountered along the way, and, ultimately, the triumph of overcoming these challenges.

Let's illustrate this strategy with a challenging example. Imagine that you are presenting the benefits of a new software solution for streamlining workflows. Instead of simply listing features and benefits (which c an b e i ncredibly d ry), t ry f raming it as a story. You might want to introduce a relatable character–perhaps a frustrated manager overwhelmed by inefficient processes. Then you depict the struggles this manager faces, the lost productivity, the missed deadlines. This sets the scene and builds empathy with the audience. The rising action involves the introduction of your new software solution. The climax is when the software streamlines the whole process, and the resolution depicts the positive outcomes–increased productivity, happier employees, improved profits, and a less stressed manager. This transforms a technical presentation into a compelling human story.

Master the art of the pause

This is often overlooked but an incredibly effective part of public speaking. Strategic pauses can create emphasis, allow audience engagement, and/or give you a moment to gather your thoughts if you feel overwhelmed. These pauses can also let your audience process information further. Don't be afraid of silence during a presentation; it can be a powerful tool; embrace it.

Visual aids

This is another important element of engaging presentations. They enhance comprehension, improve retention. However, it's essential to use visual aids strategically. Avoid overwhelming your audience with too much text on each slide; use concise bullet points and impactful imagery (when necessary). High-quality visuals–sharp images, well-designed graphs, and charts–add professionalism and credibility to your presentation. Use visuals to illustrate your points, emphasize key messages, and break up long stretches of text.

Compelling visuals should be more than mere decorations; they should be integral to your message. They should work in harmony with your words, not compete with them. Every visual should have a clear purpose, reinforcing your key messages and making the information easier to understand and remember. Avoid cluttered slides, which can overwhelm your audience with too much information at once. Keep your slides clean, focused, and easy on the eyes.

Embrace imperfections

Like any skill, public speaking requires practice and refinement. Don't expect perfection on your first attempt or even your tenth. Accept that there will be moments where you stumble. You could forget a point, misspeak, or something happens out of your control, like a technology failure. These are all part of the process of learning and getting better. Adjust your approach and continue to hone your skills. View each presentation as a learning opportunity.

Structure

A well-structured presentation follows a logical flow, ensuring your points are presented clearly and cohesively. A clear introduction sets the stage, outlining your objectives and grabbing the audience's attention. The body of your presentation should develop your ideas logically and progressively. A firm conclusion summarizes your key points and leaves a lasting impression.

Word choice and delivery

The words you choose and how you express them are pivotal in communication. Your tone, pace, and body language significantly influence the impact of your message. Thoughtful and intentional language can inspire and motivate listeners, creating a solid connection and encouraging them to act. On the other hand, careless or poorly chosen words can lead to misunderstandings, confusion, and damage your credibility. This emphasizes the importance of being mindful about communication in personal and professional settings.

Moreover, effective public speaking goes beyond mere word choice. Practicing and refining your skills can enhance your ability to convey your message clearly and resonate with your audience. The delivery of your message, including your confidence and authenticity, can elevate its power. When you engage your audience through eye contact, appropriate gestures, and a steady pace, you deepen their investment in your words. Ultimately, harnessing the impact of language and delivery enables you to share your ideas more effectively and helps you build trust and rapport with those you wish to influence.

MASTERING THE Q&A

You've delivered a compelling presentation, weaving a narrative that captivated your audience and now you must navigate the transition from your structured presentation to the unpredictable terrain of the Q&A session. This is where many presentations falter. While not every presentation needs a Q&A, it is nevertheless an essential part of many presentations to field questions and concerns from the audience. These sessions separate the successful and merely competent speakers. Mastering the Q&A is not about having all the answers—it's about handling the questions with grace, intelligence, and, crucially, maintaining control of the narrative.

The Q&A session is a crucial extension of your presentation, a chance to solidify your message further and establish yourself as a thought leader. It's a high-stakes arena, where one poorly handled question can unravel the positive momentum you have built.

Preparation

The first (and most obvious) strategy is preparation. But this isn't just about anticipating potential questions; it's about crafting a plan to handle any question, expected or not. Start by brainstorming. What are the common misconceptions or ambiguities surrounding your topic? What are the potential points of contention? Write these down. Then, formulate clear, concise, and insightful answers to each. Don't memorize the answers verbatim–instead, internalize the key points and practice articulating them in different ways. This flexibility is crucial for handling unexpected variations of your anticipated questions.

Consider creating a "cheat sheet," not with answers but key talking points organized around potential themes. This allows you to stay focused on the message even if the question takes you slightly off track. For example, suppose your presentation focused on the benefits of implementing a new project management system. In that case, your cheat sheet might list key metrics, success stories from pilot programs, and strategies for addressing resistance to change.

View the Q&A as an opportunity

Beyond anticipating specific questions (and their variations), cultivate a mindset of welcoming them. Frame the Q&A session as a valuable dialogue, as each question is an opportunity to deepen engagement and strengthen your connection with the audience. A simple yet powerful technique is to start your response by acknowledging and validating the question. For example, instead of directly answering a challenging question about the cost of a new initiative, you might say, "That's a fundamental question that deserves careful consideration. The cost implications are indeed significant, but..." This buys you time to formulate a thoughtful response and signals to the audience that you are taking their concerns seriously and are listening to them as they are listening to you.

Stay focused

Handling difficult qu estions re quires fin esse. Som e questions might be aggressive, challenging your expertise or even your integrity. Reacting defensively is tempting, but doing so will often un-dermine your credibility. Instead, maintain your composure. Please take a deep breath, acknowledge the question calmly, and reframe it as necessary. Don't hesitate to ask for clarification if a question is un-clear or ambiguous. This allows you to ensure that you address the actual concern, rather than a misinterpretation. Remember, this ses-sion is an opportunity to connect with the audience and quell any misunderstandings or problems.

For questions (or comments) that directly challenge your assertions, avoid getting into a debate. Instead, reiterate your key points using different l anguage o r e xamples. I f t he q uestion i s o utside the scope of your presentation, acknowledge its validity and politely offer to follow up later, providing contact information or suggesting relevant resources. This demonstrates professionalism and avoids getting bogged down in tangents distracting your main message.

Be mindful of body language

Maintain eye contact with the person asking the question, even if you need a moment to gather your thoughts. Use open and welcoming postures to project confidence. Avoid fidgeting or nervously shifting your weight. A calm and composed demeanor will reassure the audience and demonstrate mastery of the subject. Even if you don't know the answer immediately, your poise will communicate your competence and willingness to address the issue thoughtfully.

Manage the flow

Managing the flow of the Q&A session is critical. If time is limited, politely but firmly guide the conversation. You might say, "We only have a few minutes left, so let's focus on the most pressing questions." Or, if several people are vying to ask questions, establish a fair system for selecting participants. This ensures everyone feels heard without derailing your schedule.

When the Q&A session ends, thank the audience for their insightful questions, reaffirm your key message, and leave a lasting impression. Remember, the Q&A session is about so much more than just answering questions; it's about transforming the opportunity into a dynamic engagement that reinforces your authority, strengthens your message, and solidifies your leadership position. The ability to confidently and effectively handle questions separates the good presenter from the great communicator. This leader truly connects with their audience. The more you practice, the more naturally this will flow, turning what might seem daunting into a powerful tool in your leadership arsenal.

Public speaking is an essential skill for any professional, especially for leaders. By employing the strategies outlined in this section, you can overcome your stage fright (if you have it), create an engaging and insightful presentation, and ace the Q&A session. By mastering public speaking, you'll not just deliver a presentation; you'll inspire, motivate, and lead with undeniable impact. The journey to commanding attention isn't just about the technology you use or the visuals you create; it's about connecting with your audience on a deeply human level, building bridges of trust and understanding, and leading them toward a shared vision. The ability to speak in front of an audience and persuade them is a genuinely impactful leadership skill, the key that unlocks the potential for positive change and enduring success. It's the ability to translate knowledge into action and vision into reality. It's the art of not just speaking but of genuinely connecting.

CHAPTER 6

Motivating and Leading Others

Become the kind of leader that people would follow voluntarily; even if you had no title or position.
-Brian Tracy

Motivating a team isn't about wielding authority; it's about igniting a fire within each individual, promoting a shared vision, and empowering them to put their best foot forward. Effective communication is the oxygen to that fire. It's the bridge that connects your vision to their actions, transforming a collection of individuals into a cohesive, high-performing unit. Think of an orchestra; each musician plays their part, but the magic is created when they play *together*. And all of this is possible because of the conductor running the show.

This harmonious collaboration starts with understanding what truly motivates your team members. Are they driven by recognition? Do they thrive on challenges? Are they intrinsically motivated by the work itself, or are they more externally focused on rewards and compensation? Understanding these key motivators is crucial. A "one size fits all" approach to motivation will not work. What inspires one person might demotivate another. That is why the main key to motivating a team is to first understand each individual's motivator, then attack that approach.

But how does a leader figure out what motivates their team? There are a few models and theories that can help us here.

Maslow's Hierarchy of Needs

This is a pyramid-shaped model that depicts human needs in a hierarchical order developed by Abraham Maslow in 1943 [16]. The bottom tier represents basic physiological needs like food and shelter, followed by safety and security. As we progress up the pyramid, we encounter social needs like love and belonging that make us feel welcome, esteem needs that drive us to achieve and gain recognition, and finally, self actualization needs that fuel our desire for personal growth.

Understanding this hierarchy allows leaders to identify the needs of their team members and tailor their approach accordingly. For instance, a team member struggling with work-life balance might be seeking fulfillment in their social needs (middle tier), while another might be driven by esteem needs–the need for recognition and achievement (second tier).

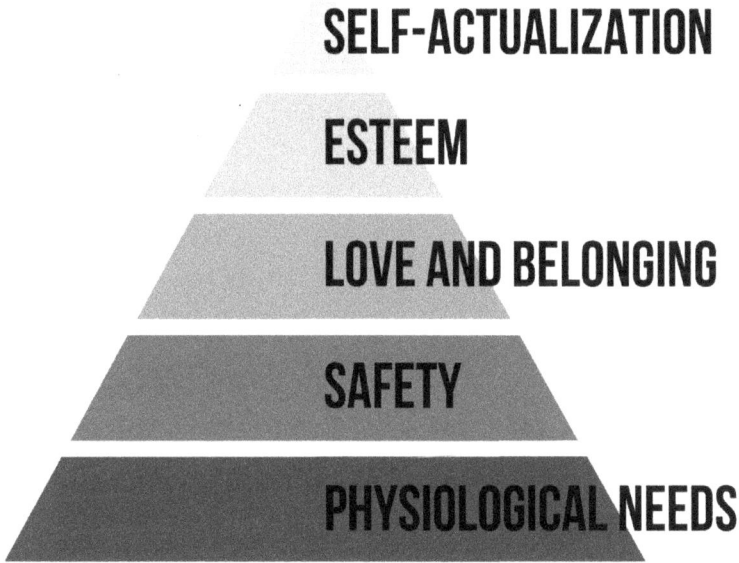

SELF-ACTUALIZATION

ESTEEM

LOVE AND BELONGING

SAFETY

PHYSIOLOGICAL NEEDS

Herzberg's Two-Factor Theory

This theory distinguishes between hygiene factors, which prevent dissatisfaction, and motivators, which drive satisfaction [17]. Hygiene factors, such as salary and working conditions, are essential to prevent discontent but don't actually inspire employees. On the other hand, motivators like achievement, recognition, and responsibility can ignite a spark or motivation and lead to increased performance.

HYGIENE FACTORS

SALARY
JOB SECURITY
STATUS
WORK CONDITIONS
RELATIONSHIPS

MOTIVATION FACTORS

ACHIEVEMENT
RECOGNITION
ADVANCEMENT
GROWTH
RESPONSIBILITY

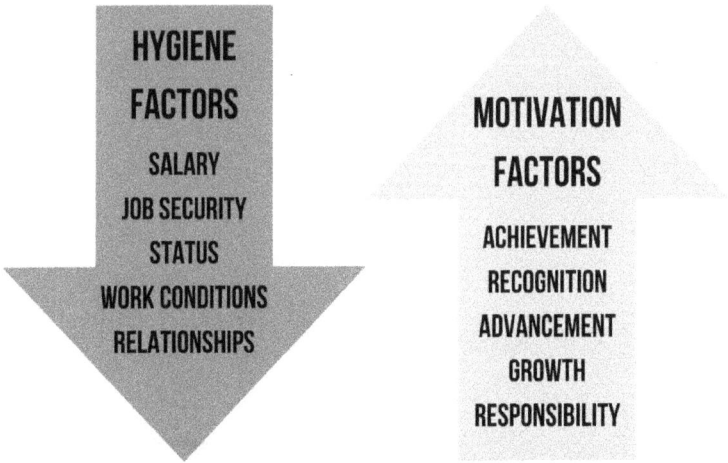

Goal Setting Theory

This emphasizes the importance of clear, challenging, and specific goals in motivating individuals [18]. When employees understand what they're working towards and have a stake in achieving it, their motivation and engagement soar. This theory also highlights the importance of feedback, which provides employees with a clear understanding of their progress and helps them stay on track.

Expectancy Theory

This theory states that individuals are motivated when they believe their effort will lead to desired outcomes and that these outcomes are valuable [19]. This theory underscores the belief that increased effort will lead to desired outcomes (expectancy), that performance benchmarks being met will lead to rewards (instrumentality), and that the rewards associated with achieving these goals are valuable to the individual (valency).

EXPECTANCY	INSTRUMENTALITY	VALENCY
EFFORT	PERFORMANCE	REWARDS

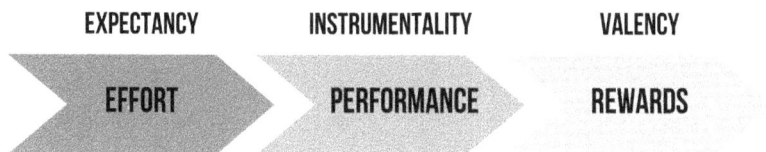

Equity Theory

The equity theory focuses on the perceived fairness of rewards and contributions [20]. Individuals compare their inputs and outputs of others in their team. If they perceive an imbalance, it can lead to decreased motivation and engagement. Leaders should strive to maintain a sense of fairness and ensure that rewards are aligned with contributions.

HOW TO CREATE A CULTURE WHERE TEAM MEMBERS CAN THRIVE

As a leader, your role is to identify the strengths and motivations of each team member, understand their unique needs and aspirations, and provide the right conditions for them to thrive. This involves:

Creating a sense of purpose

Creating a sense of purpose is key to building a high-performing team. Clearly articulate the team's goals, values, and mission. This provides a North Star that guides everyone's efforts and decisions. When people understand the "why" behind their work, they become more engaged and motivated.

You also need to help your team understand how their individual contributions build into the greater good. Every role, no matter how big or small, plays a part in achieving the team's objectives. By highlighting these connections, you can encourage a sense of pride and ownership. People are more likely to go the extra mile when they see how their work impacts the bigger picture.

By creating a strong sense of purpose, you can unlock your team's full potential and achieve great things together. It's the foundation upon which all else is built. So take the time to clearly define your team's purpose and help everyone see their part in the mission.

Providing recognition and appreciation

Acknowledge and celebrate team members' achievements, both big and small.

Imagine a team member who has worked tirelessly on a challenging project, pulling late nights and putting in extra effort to meet a tight deadline. They finally deliver a successful product, exceeding expectations. What do you do?

A simple "good job" won't cut it here. Instead, take the time to acknowledge their specific contributions and the impact they have made. For instance, you could say "I want to thank you for your incredible work on this project. Your dedication and problem-solving skills were crucial to the success of this launch. You went above and beyond, and it didn't go unnoticed. You truly made a difference."

This kind of recognition goes beyond simply acknowledging their effort; it focuses on the specific impact they have made.

Empowering autonomy

Empowering autonomy is a powerful way to unlock your team's potential. Give team members the freedom to make decisions and take ownership of their work. When people feel trusted and empowered, they become more engaged and motivated. Micromanaging, on the other hand, can lead to disengagement and resentment against leadership.

Empowering team members with autonomy creates a sense of responsibility and encourages initiative. When team members have this freedom to approach tasks in their own way, they're more likely to take pride in their work and strive for excellence. Autonomy also promotes and exercises their problem solving skills, as they are free to experiment and try new approaches.

However, autonomy *without guidance* can lead to confusion and misalignment. Clearly define the boundaries and expectations, then let them take it from there. Provide the necessary resources and support, but let the team determine the *how.* You also must celebrate successes and learn from failures as a team, using them as opportunities for growth.

By empowering autonomy, you can create a culture of ownership and accountability. People will rise to the level of trust you place in them. So delegate effectively, provide feedback rather than direction, and watch your team soar. With autonomy, purpose, and the right support, there is no limit to what you can achieve together.

Providing meaningful feedback

Providing meaningful feedback is important for team member growth and development. Offer regular feedback, both positive and constructive, that is specific, actionable, and focused on growth. Instead of saying a simple "good job on the project" you could say something like "I really appreciated how you broke down the complex problem into manageable parts and kept us on track . Your project management skills are a huge asset to our team."

You must provide guidance and support to help team members overcome obstacles and develop their skills. Constructive feedback should never leave someone feeling deflated or unclear on how to improve. Instead pair it with specific recommendations and resources for growth. For instance, if someone is struggling with public speaking, you could connect them with a workshop to provide tips on preparation and practice. Celebrate wins and progress along the way to keep motivation high.

However, feedback, like any skill, takes time to master. Be timely, specific, and sincere in your delivery. Avoid generic praise or criticism, and instead focus on observable behaviors and their impact. Ask open-ended questions to encourage self-reflection and ownership of growth. By doing so, you'll help your team members become more aware of their strengths and areas for development.

Feedback is the bridge between where people are, and where they can be. Make it a regular part of your leadership practice, and watch your team thrive. And remember, the goal of feedback is growth, not criticism. Approach it with empathy and a mindset tuned for growth and you will create a culture where people feel safe to take calculated risks and strive for excellence.

Fostering a supportive environment

Another key of building a high-performance team is cultivating a supportive environment in your organization. This is done by creating a work environment that is inclusive, respectful, and values collaboration. When people feel safe and valued, they're much more likely to speak up, share ideas, and support each other. This leads to better decision making and problem solving.

But, a supportive environment doesn't mean avoiding tough conversations of conflicts altogether. Address issues head on, but do so with empathy and respect. Focus on finding solutions rather than placing blame. By doing so, you'll create trust and demonstrate that everyone's voice matters. Lead by example, treating others with kindness, respect, and consideration.

Remember, motivation is not a one-size-fits-all approach. You need to understand the unique needs and aspirations of each individual and create the conditions for them to thrive.

THE POWER OF EQ

Emotional intelligence, often referred to as EQ (which stands for emotional quotient), is a powerful tool that can transform your leadership style. EQ is the ability to not only understand and manage your own emotions, but also to recognize and respond effectively to the emotions of others. In the realm of leadership, emotional intelligence becomes a vital ingredient for inspiring, motivating, and building strong, cohesive teams. It is the glue that holds your team together, enabling you to forge meaningful connections and guide them towards shared goals.

Imagine leading a team through a challenging project. Deadlines are looming, pressure is mounting, and team members are starting to feel overwhelmed. Without emotional intelligence, you might resort to giving harsh commands, dismissing their concerns, or even resorting to blaming others. This approach only exacerbates the situation, creating resentment and hindering the team's progress.

However, a leader with high emotional intelligence would approach the situation in a completely different manner. They would start by acknowledging the team's feelings, creating a safe space for open communication, and showing empathy for their challenges. They would listen intently to their perspectives, and offer support. Instead of resorting to pressuring their team to meet the upcoming deadlines, they would focus on finding creative solutions collaboratively.

Developing emotional intelligence isn't about becoming a mind reader, it's about cultivating self-awareness and actively listening to others. It is about building empathy and understanding, enabling you to connect with your team members on a deeper level.

Here are actionable strategies to enhance your emotional intelligence and inspire your team:

SELF AWARENESS

Reflect on your own emotions

Take time to observe and understand your own emotional responses. What triggers your emotions? How do you typically react under pressure? Identifying your emotional patterns will help you manage them more effectively.

Practice mindfulness

Mindfulness techniques like meditation or deep breathing exercises can help you become more aware of your thoughts, feelings, and reactions. This practice will enable you to respond to situations with greater clarity and composure.

Seek feedback

Ask trusted colleagues, friends, or mentors for feedback on your emotional intelligence. How do your actions impact others? Are you perceived as empathetic, understanding, and approachable? Be open to constructive criticism and use it to refine your EQ.

EMPATHY AND UNDERSTANDING

Active listening

Listen attentively to your team members, and pay attention to their words, tone of voice, and body language. Try to see the situation from their perspective.

Ask questions

Don't just assume that you understand what your team members are saying. Ask open-ended questions to give them a chance to clarify their thoughts, feelings, and concerns.

Validate their feelings

Acknowledge and validate the emotions your team members express, even if you don't agree with their perspective. A simple phrase like "I understand you're feeling frustrated" can go a long way in building trust and creating a safe space for open communication.

EMOTIONAL REGULATION

Manage your stress

Chronic stress can negatively impact your emotional intelligence. Find healthy ways to manage stress, such as exercise, relaxation techniques, or spending time doing what you love.

Practice patience

Don't rush to judgment or react impulsively. Take a moment to breathe and collect your thoughts before responding to a challenging situation.

Be aware of your triggers

Recognize your emotional triggers and develop strategies for coping with them. If you know that a particular topic or person tends to trigger your emotions, be prepared to manage your reactions and remain composed.

BUILDING RELATIONSHIPS

Show appreciation

Express gratitude for your team members' contributions, both big and small. A sincere thank you or simple act of recognition goes a long way in boosting morale and strengthening relationships.

Create a culture of trust

Create a workplace environment where team members feel safe to share their thoughts, feelings, and concerns without fear of judgment. Be open and transparent in your communication, and be willing to apologize when you make mistakes.

Invest in team building

Organize team-building activities that promote communication, collaboration, and camaraderie. Shared experiences can help team members connect on a deeper level and build trust.

Emotional intelligence is a cornerstone of effective leadership. It is the ability to connect with your team on a human level, understand their needs, and inspire them to achieve their full potential. By cultivating empathy, managing your emotions effectively, and building stronger relationships, you can create a positive and productive work environment that upholds growth and achievement.

Remember, emotional intelligence is a skill that can be developed over time. Through self-reflection, mindful practice, and a genuine desire to connect with others, you can become a more empathetic and effective leader, inspiring your team to reach new heights.

CHAPTER 7

Coaching and Mentoring

I start with the premise that the function of leadership is to produce more leaders, not more followers.
-Ralph Nader

Building upon the principles of motivating and leading others, we will now explore the art of effective coaching before diving into the art of effective mentoring.

Coaching and mentoring are often used interchangeably, but they represent distinct approaches to leadership development. Understanding their nuances is imperative for building a robust framework that builds growth within your organization. While both aim to improve performance and develop skills, their methodologies and focuses differ significantly.

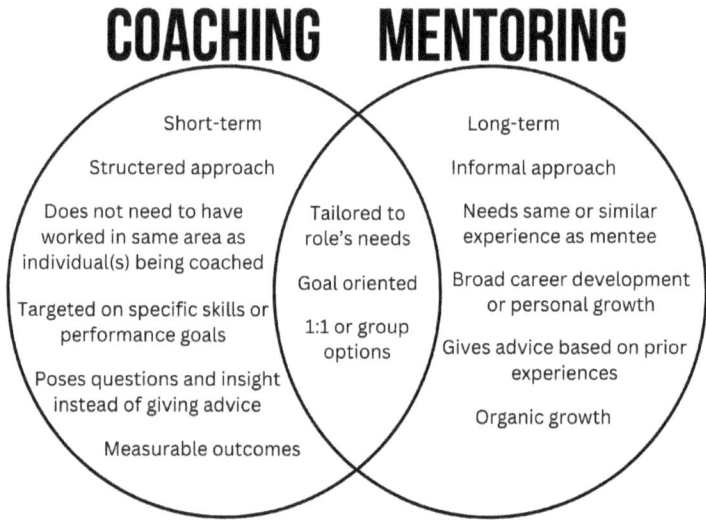

COACHING MENTORING

COACHING side:
- Short-term
- Structered approach
- Does not need to have worked in same area as individual(s) being coached
- Targeted on specific skills or performance goals
- Poses questions and insight instead of giving advice
- Measurable outcomes

Overlap (center):
- Tailored to role's needs
- Goal oriented
- 1:1 or group options

MENTORING side:
- Long-term
- Informal approach
- Needs same or similar experience as mentee
- Broad career development or personal growth
- Gives advice based on prior experiences
- Organic growth

COACHING

Coaching is a more targeted, short-term process focused on specific skills or performance goals. A coach works with an individual to identify performance gaps, develop actionable plans to address these gaps and track progress toward achieving predetermined objectives. The coach is a facilitator, guiding the individual through self-discovery and problem-solving. The relationship is typically more structured, with regular meetings and measurable outcomes. Being a coach in the world of business is very similar in many ways to being a sports coach–both provide specific training and guidance to help the team members improve their performance through regular meetings and actionable goals.

As a leader, you should think of coaching not as a top-down directive but as a collaborative partnership focused on unlocking individual potential. It's about empowering your team members to identify their strengths, overcome weaknesses, and ultimately achieve their professional aspirations. This isn't simply about providing solutions; it's about guiding them to discover their own. This boosts self-reliance and a sense of ownership in their growth.

One of the foundational elements of effective coaching is understanding the diverse coaching styles that can be employed. The "tell-sell" approach, while seemingly straightforward, can be counterproductive. This method, characterized by delivering solutions directly without exploring the team's perspective, often leaves team members feeling disempowered and potentially resentful. Imagine a scenario where a team member struggles with a complex project. A tell-sell approach might involve dictating a precise solution, bypassing the opportunity to understand the root cause of the struggle and thereby missing the chance to address the underlying skill gaps.

Instead, employ the power of active listening. Before offering guidance, genuinely listen to your team member's concerns, challenges, and perspectives. Ask probing questions to uncover the underlying issues, demonstrating your genuine interest in their development. This approach will build trust and open communication, creating a safe space where individuals feel comfortable sharing their vulnerabilities without fear of judgment. For instance, if a team member expresses frustration with a particular task, instead of immediately offering solutions, ask questions like "Can you tell me more about what's challenging you?" or "What have you tried so far?" This lets you grasp the situation from their viewpoint before offering advice.

The power of questioning is paramount in coaching. Rather than providing direct answers, skillfully crafted questions can guide team members toward self-discovery and problem-solving. Open-ended questions such as "What are your thoughts on...?" or "How might we approach this differently?" encourage critical thinking and self-reflection. This approach facilitates a shift from dependence to independence, nurturing the individual's ability to analyze situations, formulate solutions, and take ownership of their development.

Another coaching model is the **GROW** model. This widely used framework guides the coaching conversation through four key stages: **G**oal, **R**eality, **O**ptions, and **W**ill. The first step is helping the team members identify a clear, achievable goal and explore the current reality, examine strengths and weaknesses, and identify obstacles. Together, they will then brainstorm potential options and strategies to overcome these obstacles. Finally, they will work together to develop a plan of action, ensuring the individual has the "will" and commitment to implement the chosen strategies.

There are a plethora of coaching strategies, and the selection of a particular model depends on the individual's needs and specific challenges.

It is also important to tailor your coaching approach to the individual. What works for one person might not work for another. Consider personality types, learning styles, and individual goals when crafting your coaching strategy. Some individuals thrive in structured environments with clear goals and expectations. In contrast, others prefer a more flexible approach with ample room for exploration. Adaptability is key–a skilled coach will adjust their style to meet the unique needs of each team member. But how do you determine the team members' learning styles to select a coaching style that will work well for them? Luckily, there are a few methods for this.

METHODS TO ASSESS LEARNING STYLES: SELF-ASSESSMENT TOOLS

Learning Style Inventories

Distribute questionnaires or online assessments that ask employees to identify their preferred learning modalities (visual, auditory, kinesthetic, or a combination)

Personality Tests

Tools like the Myers-Briggs Type Indicator (MBTI) can provide insights into cognitive preferences, which can inform learning style assessments [21].

Workplace behavior

Observe how team members approach tasks and challenges. Do they prefer visual aids, hands-on activities, or verbal explanations?

Training Preferences

Note the types of training programs that employees respond to best. Do they prefer in-person workshops, online courses, or self-paced learning?

Direct Questions

Ask employees directly about their preferred learning style. "How do you typically learn new information most effectively?"

Past Learning Experiences

Discuss past training experiences to identify successful and unsuccessful approaches.

Experiment with Different Approaches

Try different training methods (in-person, virtual, blended) and measure their effectiveness.

Iterate and Improve

Use the insights gained from pilot programs to refine future training initiatives.

Learning Management Systems (LMS)

Utilize LMS data to track employee engagement with different learning modalities.

Performance Metrics

Correlate learning style preferences with employee learning metrics to identify potential correlations.

Furthermore, effective coaching goes beyond one-on-one sessions. It encompasses providing ongoing support and encouragement, offering regular check-ins to monitor progress, and providing constructive feedback on performance. This demonstrates your commitment to their development and reinforces the value you place on their contributions to the team. Regular check-ins also allow for ongoing support and adjustments, ensuring the coaching process remains relevant and impactful.

Goal setting is another powerful tool in coaching. Collaboratively establish specific, measurable, relevant, and time-bound **(SMART)** goals. This gives the team member a clear direction and purpose, providing a tangible framework for their development. Regularly review progress toward these goals, celebrating achievements and adjusting the plan as needed. This continuous feedback loop keeps the individual motivated and engaged in the process.

Another effective technique is role-playing. This involves simulating real-life scenarios, allowing the individual to practice specific skills in a safe and supportive environment. This method is particularly effective in developing communication skills, negotiation tactics, or conflict resolution strategies. By role-playing, individuals can experiment with different approaches, receive constructive feedback, and build confidence in their abilities to handle challenging scenarios.

MENTORING

Conversely, mentoring is a longer-term, more relational process focused on b rœder career development and personal growth. A mentor acts as a guide and advisor, sharing their experience, wisdom, and network to support the mentee's overall professional journey. The relationship is often less structured (although structured mentorship programs exist; more on that later), allowing for greater flexibility and organic growth. A mentor might guide career paths, offer insights into organizational politics, or help the mentee navigate challenging situations. The mentorship focuses on development, encompassing professional skills and personal attributes such as leadership, resilience, and emotional intelligence. Consider a mentor as a seasoned explorer guiding a younger explorer through unfamiliar territory–offering insights, warnings, and support.

The distinction between coaching and mentoring is not always clear-cut; there can b e considerable overlap (as visualized by our Venn diagram at the beginning of the chapter). A mentor might utilize coaching techniques to help the mentee address specific challenges, while a coach might offer broader career advice based on their experience. The most effective leadership development programs often integrate coaching and mentoring approaches, leveraging each other's strengths to maximize individual growth. The key is to understand the individual's specific needs and tailor the approach accordingly.

Building strong mentoring relationships hinges on establishing trust, mutual respect, and shared goals. It's a dynamic partnership, not a hierarchical one, where the mentor and mentee contribute actively to the relationship's success. The effectiveness of mentoring isn't solely dependent on the mentor's experience; it's equally influenced by the mentee's willingness to learn, actively participate, and embrace feedback. This collaborative spirit is crucial for navigating the complexities and achieving mutually beneficial outcomes.

The first practical step in a mentorship is clearly defining expectations. This involves setting realistic goals, establishing a communication plan, and outlining the roles and responsibilities of each participant. Open and honest communication prevents misunderstandings and lays the groundwork for a productive relationship. A formal agreement, whether written or verbal, outlining meeting frequencies, the scope of the mentoring relationship, and expectations regarding confidentiality, is highly beneficial. This ensures transparency and provides a reference point throughout this journey.

The frequency and format of the meetings should be tailored to the needs of both the mentor and mentee. Some pairs prefer weekly meetings, while others might find monthly sessions more manageable. The format of these meetings could be structured discussions based on predetermined agendas or more open-ended conversations focusing on immediate challenges or opportunities. The most effective approach involves a blend of both structured and informal interactions. Structured meetings ensure that key areas are addressed, while informal conversations foster a more natural and comfortable exchange, encouraging more open dialogue and trust.

Effective mentoring extends beyond formal meetings. It involves providing constructive feedback, actively listening, and offering support and encouragement when needed. Feedback should be specific, actionable, and delivered in a timely and sensitive manner. It's about fostering growth, not criticism. Active listening, a foundation of leadership communication, as it interweaves into every single lesson in these pages, is integral here to demonstrate respect and a genuine interest in the mentee's progress. Mentors should create a safe space for mentees to share their thoughts and feelings without judgment.

This trust is essential for the mentee to be vulnerable and honest, which is crucial for meaningful personal and professional growth.

IMPLEMENTING A STRUCTURED MENTORSHIP PROGRAM

A structured mentorship program ensures consistency and maximizes results. Here are the steps to build a successful mentorship program:

First, define clear objectives for the program. Whether the goals are skill-building, leadership development, or career advancement, having well-defined objectives ensures that both mentors and mentees understand the purpose and direction of the program.

Next, match mentors and mentees thoughtfully. This can be achieved using surveys or interviews to pair individuals based on compatibility. Aligning interests, goals, and personalities can significantly enhance the effectiveness of the mentorship relationship.

Once pairs are established, set clear expectations. Establishing defined roles and responsibilities for mentors and mentees, along with measurable outcomes, helps maintain focus and accountability throughout the mentorship journey.

Providing the necessary resources is crucial for effective mentorship. Equip mentors with tools and training that will aid them in offering valuable guidance and support. This could include training workshops, resource materials, or network access and opportunities.

Regular check-ins are essential to foster accountability and address any challenges that may arise. Schedule consistent meetings where mentors and mentees can discuss progress, set new goals, and troubleshoot any issues together.

Evaluating the program's success is vital. Gather mentor and mentee feedback and use performance metrics to assess the program's effectiveness. This data can be used to refine and improve the program over time.

Finally, cultivate a supportive culture within the organization. Celebrate successful mentor-mentee relationships and encourage a culture of knowledge-sharing and collaboration. Highlighting success stories and acknowledging achievements can motivate others to participate and engage more deeply with the program.

A structured mentorship program provides a framework for growth while maintaining flexibility to meet individual needs, ensuring that mentors and mentees benefit from the experience.

MAINTAINING MOTIVATION IN LONG-TERM RELATIONSHIPS

Long-term coaching relationships require intentional strategies to remain effective and engaging. Here are some tips to sustain engagement over time:

Set milestones

Breaking down long-term goals into smaller, achievable steps can make the journey less daunting and more manageable. Celebrating these small wins can keep motivation high and provide a sense of progress.

Add variety to the relationship

Alternate between different activities such as discussions, workshops, or collaborative projects. This variety can keep interactions fresh and exciting, preventing monotony and maintaining interest.

Regularly update goals

Revisit and update goals to remain relevant and aligned with the mentor's and mentee's evolving needs and aspirations This keeps the relationship dynamic and goal-oriented.

Encourage autonomy in the mentee

Empowering individuals to take charge of their development fosters independence and self-motivation. Please provide them with the necessary tools and support, but allow them the freedom to explore and grow.

Promote mutual learning within the relationship

Create opportunities for mentors and mentees to share insights and learn from each other. This reciprocal exchange of knowledge can enrich both parties' experiences.

Foster personal connections beyond professional roles

Taking the time to understand and appreciate each other personally can deepen the relationship and build trust, making the mentoring experience more meaningful.

Utilize feedback loops to adapt and improve the relationship continuously

Regularly seek feedback and be open to making changes based on the insights gained. This helps ensure that the relationship remains productive and fulfilling.

Offer tangible benefits linked to growth

Connect the progress made in the mentoring relationship to real-world opportunities such as promotions, certifications, or new responsib ilities. This demonstrates the practical value of the relationship and motivates ongoing engagement.

Sustaining engagement in long-term mentoring relationships ensures that mentors and mentees continue to find value and benefit from their interactions, ultimately leading to personal and professional growth.

FOSTERING A CULTURE OF LEARNING AND GROWTH

A culture of learning and growth transforms organizations. Individuals collectively strengthen the team when they view challenges as opportunities and prioritize knowledge-sharing.

Encouraging team members to collaborate, share training insights, and offer constructive feedback breeds innovation. A growth-oriented culture empowers employees to take initiative, speak up, and contribute meaningfully to the organization's success.

Coaching and mentoring are transformative leadership tools that build resilient, capable teams. Leaders can inspire lasting development by understanding individual learning styles, providing tailored feedback, and fostering a culture of trust and growth. A commitment to mentoring creates a ripple effect, benefiting individuals, organizations, and communities alike.

CHAPTER 8

Giving and Receiving Feedback

Accept both compliments and criticism. It takes both sun and rain for a flower to grow.
-Marek Kośniowski

Feedback serves as an essential catalyst for growth and development, benefiting individuals and organizations alike. For leaders, the ability to deliver and receive feedback effectively transcends being merely a useful skill; it is a fundamental requirement for successful leadership. Feedback acts as a guiding light, providing clarity and direction that empower leaders to adjust their strategies, expand their skill sets, and lead with purpose and intention.

True leadership is best illustrated by a commitment to continual progress rather than a relentless pursuit of perfection. By embracing feedback—whether it comes in the form of accolades or constructive criticism—leaders create a nurturing environment that not only promotes individual and collective growth but also fuels innovation and paves the way for sustained success.

WHY FEEDBACK MATTERS FOR LEADERS

Feedback helps individuals learn from experiences, identify strengths, and improve. For leaders, a strong feedback system enhances their ability to lead effectively, drives innovation within their teams, and nurtures a culture of continuous improvement. Effective feedback flows in all directions—top-down, bottom-up, and peer-to-peer. This inclusive approach ensures leaders remain connected with their teams, valued, and empowered to guide the organization toward success.

One essential element of effective leadership is how feedback is given and received. Communication plays a pivotal role in engaging and retaining team members. Implementing regular feedback loops can create an environment where leaders feel comfortable sharing their thoughts and receiving constructive feedback. This practice is proven to improve leadership effectiveness and boost team morale, creating a more cohesive and committed workforce [22].

Regular feedback loops involve continuous interactions where feedback is shared consistently rather than sporadically. This ongoing process allows for real-time adjustments and reinforces a culture of openness. For example, scheduling regular check-ins between leaders and their teams can foster a more dynamic and responsive work environment. These sessions provide opportunities to address issues promptly, celebrate successes, and set new goals, enhancing a leader's ability to adapt and respond to the team's needs.

Feedback loops also play a vital role in a leader's development. When leaders receive timely and specific feedback, they better understand their performance and areas that need improvement. This clarity enables them to make informed decisions about their professional growth and leadership style. Specific, focused feedback can significantly impact a leader's effectiveness. Leaders can continuously enhance their skills and productivity by setting clear expectations and providing actionable feedback.

Beyond individual growth, regular feedback loops can significantly impact team dynamics. When team members share feedback with leaders, they better understand each other's strengths and challenges, leading to more effective teamwork. Implementing regular inter-departmental meetings where feedback is shared can align goals and strategies, fostering a more cohesive and efficient working environment.

Recognizing achievements through feedback also boosts morale and motivation, encouraging leaders and their teams to strive for excellence. A Gallup survey reported that employees who feel recognized are 2.5 times as likely to be happy at their jobs and 1.5 times as likely to feel motivated to do their best [23].

Celeb rating successes acknowledges individual contributions and reinforces positive behaviors. A formal system for recognizing accomplishments, such as regular team meetings or "employee of the month" programs, can significantly enhance workplace morale and motivation.

Implementing regular feedback loops helps leaders create a more engaging and collaborative work environment. It also retains team members, boosts morale, and enhances individual and team performance. Regular feedback ensures continuous improvement, fosters a culture of openness, and drives overall leadership effectiveness.

WHY FEEDBACK IS IMPERATIVE FOR LEADERSHIP DEVELOPMENT

A robust feedback culture benefits leaders by promoting their growth and development. Constructive feedback helps leaders improve their skills and advance professionally. Research demonstrates that feedback interventions can significantly impact performance, especially when the feedback is specific and focuses on improvement areas. Regular one-on-one meetings where leaders receive tailored feedback ensure that feedback is timely, relevant, and focused on individual development, leading to continuous leadership improvement.

Effective feedback enhances a leader's communication skills by clarifying expectations, resolving concerns, and building trust. Interpersonal communication skills are crucial in fostering organizational commitment. Effective feedback improves overall communication, clarifying expectations, resolving concerns, and building trust within the team. Integrating feedback sessions into the regular workflow can prevent misunderstandings and foster a more transparent and trustful work environment.

A robust feedback culture ensures leaders understand their roles and responsibilities, leading to improved performance and accountability. By encouraging open communication and continuous improvement, leaders can build trust and commitment among their team members, ultimately driving better overall performance and innovation.

THE RISKS FOR LEADERS WHO LACK FEEDBACK

Without feedback, leaders can face significant challenges, including clarity and direction issues. Clear, specific goals are essential for high performance. Without feedback, leaders may lack the direction needed to achieve their goals. Ensuring that roles and responsibilities are clearly defined and regularly reviewed can mitigate this risk.

Moreover, leaders who do not receive feedback may feel undervalued, reducing motivation and increasing disengagement. Feedback is a critical factor in keeping leaders motivated and engaged.

Leaders not receiving regular feedback may feel their efforts go un-noticed, decreasing morale and productivity. Recognizing and ap-preciating leadership efforts regularly, seeking input, and acting on feedback can show that contributions are valued.

By understanding these risks, leaders can take proactive steps to ensure they are well-informed, motivated, and engaged, thus pre-venting potential pitfalls. Regular, constructive feedback helps maintain clarity, enhance motivation, and foster a culture of contin-uous improvement.

BUILDING A ROBUST FEEDBACK SYSTEM FOR LEADERS

A well-implemented feedback system transforms leaders by cre-ating clear expectations and accountability. Clear roles and account-ability are essential in building a committed leadership team. Leaders are more likely to be engaged and committed when they understand their roles and are held accountable for their performance. Regular feedback helps identify strengths and areas for improvement, foster-ing continuous growth.

Ongoing feedback is valuable for leadership performance im-provement. Regular, structured feedback helps leaders continuously develop their skills and improve performance. Building a robust feedback system involves setting clear expectations, providing regu-lar feedback, and encouraging open communication by creating safe spaces for leaders to share their thoughts and concerns.

Leaders play a critical role in modeling desired behaviors. Ac-tively seeking and giving feedback demonstrates its value. Creating a safe environment where feedback is welcomed encourages open communication. Teams perform better when they feel safe to share feedback without fear of negative consequences. Providing training on effective feedback techniques equips leaders with the skills they need to engage in meaningful feedback conversations.

Implementing a strong feedback system helps leaders build a more accountable and high-performing leadership team, ensuring continuous improvement and development. Clear expectations, regular feedback, and a safe environment for sharing thoughts contribute to a culture of openness and trust, driving overall leadership success.

PRACTICAL EXAMPLES AND BENEFITS FOR LEADERS

Consider a leader who provides regular, constructive feedback to their team. This practice helps team members improve their skills, boosting morale and productivity. Feedback interventions can significantly improve performance, especially when feedback is specific and actionable. For instance, feedback on presentation skills can help leaders enhance their delivery, leading to more impactful presentations.

Feedback also brings measurable benefits in various leadership areas. In strategic planning, adjusting feedback-based strategies can better engage stakeholders and increase overall effectiveness. Effective leadership and feedback drive success by helping teams adapt and improve continuously. Regularly collecting and acting on feedback, such as through team surveys, helps leaders adapt and improve continuously.

Regular, constructive feedback practices help leaders enhance their skills, leading to better performance and productivity. Leaders can continuously improve and adapt by regularly collecting and acting on feedback, driving overall success.

THE CALL TO ACTION FOR LEADERS

Feedback is essential for a thriving, dynamic, and resilient leadership approach. Leaders must prioritize creating systems that facilitate continuous feedback loops. Specific, a ctionable, and constructive feedback promotes growth and improvement. Setting clear guidelines ensures that feedback is helpful and promotes growth. Encouraging input across all levels empowers leaders to share ideas and concerns openly, creating a culture of continuous improvement.

Creating a feedback-friendly environment is crucial. Psychological safety is vital in fostering such an environment. When leaders feel safe to share feedback without fear of negative consequences, they are more likely to contribute openly and honestly. Acting on feedback shows that it leads to tangible improvements, reinforcing its value.

Establishing a strong feedback culture allows leaders to drive innovation, improve performance, and b uild an engaged, high-performing team. Feedback empowers leaders to reach their potential, fosters team collab oration, and drives innovation. By establishing a culture of constructive feedback, leaders can b uild stronger relationships, improve performance, and create an environment where everyone feels valued and heard.

Leaders hold the key to embedding this culture, ensuring feedback is given and acted upon meaningfully. Leaders thrive when feedback b ecomes a continuous process—flowing t op-down, bottom-up, and peer-to-peer—and their impact extends far beyond their immediate teams. Prioritizing feedback, celeb rating wins, addressing challenges, and creating a workplace where growth is encouraged and expected will pave the way for lasting success and resilience.

CHAPTER 9

Managing Difficult Conversations

When we avoid difficult conversations, we trade short-term discomfort for long-term dysfunction.
Peter Bromberg

As a leader, you will undoubtedly be tasked with navigating difficult conversations in the workplace. Whether it's addressing performance issues, resolving conflicts, or delivering tough news, these interactions can be emotionally charged and challenging to navigate. One report from *Goodpractice* found that difficult conversations are the biggest challenge faced by leaders today, with 50% of leaders citing these types of conversations as their number one challenge in the workplace [24].

The key to managing these types of conversations effectively is to understand the dynamics at play and approach them with a strategic mindset. You also have to remember that communication is a two-way street. By being a good listener, as well as being clear and concise in your message, and choosing your words carefully, you can create a more productive and positive dialogue.

One of the biggest challenges of difficult conversations is the emotional baggage they carry. Fear, anger, frustration, sadness, defensiveness are common emotions that can cloud judgment and escalate conflict. It is essential to acknowledge these emotions and understand their impact on both yourself and the other person involved.

For example, when delivering negative feedback, the recipient may feel defensive or threatened, leading to resistance or an unwillingness to listen. Similarly, when confronting a coworker about a conflict, you might feel anxious or upset, making it difficult to communicate calmly, respectfully, and with clarity.

Preparing for a difficult conversation is like preparing for a challenging hike. No hiker who cares for their safety and well-being would embark on a mountain trail without a map, comfortable hiking shoes, or water. Similarly, approaching a difficult conversation without preparation and the necessary tools can lead to misunderstandings, frustration, and a negative outcome.

The first step is to set clear objectives. What do you hope to achieve through this conversation? Do you want to resolve a conflict, deliver critical feedback, or simply gain a better understanding of someone's perspective? Defining your goals helps you stay focused and avoid veering off course during the conversation.

For example, if you're addressing a team member's poor performance, your objective might be to:

Provide specific and actionable feedback

Clearly communicate what needs improvement and offer concrete suggestions for improvement.

Establish clear expectations

Reiterate performance standards and ensure that the team member understands your expectations moving forward.

Create a plan for improvement

Collaborate on a plan to address the issues and monitor progress.

Once you have set your objectives for the conversation, choose the right time and place. A hurried talk in a crowded hallway is unlikely to be productive. Aim for a private setting where you and the other person can speak openly and without distractions. Consider the other person's schedule and availability to ensure the time chosen is convenient, and that the conversation will not be rushed.

Another key aspect of preparation is anticipating potential reactions. Put yourself in their shoes, what might your response be in that situation? What emotions would you feel? What would be going through your head? By doing this, you can better prepare yourself for how they may react, and how best to handle the situation. Always use a calm and empathetic approach when handling particularly sensitive topics (like poor performance).

If you feel like there may be resistance to your message, you could:

Start with positive affirmations

By acknowledging strengths or accomplishments first, it eases the team member into the difficult conversation, making the feedback easier to palate.

Frame feedback as a collaborative effort

Emphasize that both of you are working *together* to achieve a common goal and that your feedback is intended to support their growth and success.

Focus on behavior, not personality

Avoid making personal attacks and instead concentrate on specific actions or behaviors that need adjustment.

By taking the time to prepare for a difficult conversion, you increase your chances of having a productive and respectful dialogue. Just like a well prepared hiker navigates a challenging trail with confidence, a leader who prepares for difficult conversations is better equipped to handle them effectively and achieve a positive outcome.

MANAGING CONFLICT

Conflict is an inevitable part of human interaction, and the workplace is no exception. While conflict doesn't always have to be negative, it can quickly derail into this territory, and mitigate productivity and damage relationships. As a leader, your ability to manage conflict constructively is essential for building a cohesive and productive team.

Imagine a team tasked with launching a new product. Two team members, who have had disagreements in the past, both have a vastly different approach to their marketing strategy proposals. One favors a traditional approach, while the other favors a more progressive approach. The tension has been building steadily between them for weeks now, and without effective conflict management, this disagreement could spiral and lead to personal attacks, creating a hostile work environment and hindering progress. However, with the right approach, this conflict can become an opportunity to brainstorm creative solutions, and ultimately lead to a more robust marketing plan.

When emotions are running high, it is difficult to find common ground. The first step is to de-escalate the situation. Think of this like having the ability to calm a storm before traveling through it.

Here are some techniques to help de-escalate emotional tensions;
Active listening

Instead of immediately reacting or defending your position, actively listen to understand the other person's perspective. Put yourself in their shoes and try to see the situation from their point of view. Ask clarifying questions to ensure you understand their thoughts and concerns.

Empathy

Acknowledge the other person's feelings and validate their perspective, even if you don't agree with it. Phrases like "I understand why you feel that way," or "That must be frustrating," can go a long way in showing empathy and creating a more receptive environment.

Maintaining a calm demeanor

Your own emotions play a critical role in the situation. Maintaining a calm and composed demeanor, even if the other person is agitated. This can help de-escalate the situation and create a more conducive environment for discussion.

Taking a time out

As a last resort, if emotions are rising, and none of the other techniques have worked, don't hesitate to take a break. Suggest a brief pause to allow everyone to calm down and gather their thoughts. This can prevent the situation from spiraling out of control.

Once emotions are de-escalated, you can begin to find common ground and explore mutually beneficial solutions. This requires a collaborative approach where everyone feels heard and respected. Simply sweeping issues under the rug, or "agreeing to disagree" are mere cop-outs. Those strategies do not lead to effective solutions, rather, they save the tension and frustration for a later date. And when that wound reopens, it can become worse than before. In order to avoid this build up of tension and frustration, you must be willing to truly listen and understand the other person's perspective, as well as be able to find the common ground between your stances.

Here are some strategies for finding m utually b eneficial solutions:

Focus on shared goals

Remind everyone of the common goals and ob jctives that brought them together in the first place. This helps refocus the conversation on finding solutions that benefit the entire team.

Brainstorm creative solutions

Encourage brainstorming where everyone can contribute ideas. This helps generate a wider range of potential solutions and creates a sense of ownership among the team.

Be willing to compromise

Be flexible and willing to compromise to reach an agreement that is acceptable to everyone. Don't be afraid to let go of some of your original demands if it means finding a great solution that not only solves the problem fully, but benefits the team as a whole.

Consider trade-offs

Sometimes, finding a completely agreeable solution isn't possible. Be open to exploring compromises and trade-offs that address the key concerns of both parties.

Sometimes, conflict might devolve into personal attacks or disrespectful behavior. In these situations, it is important to address the issue directly and firmly while maintaining professionalism.

Address the behavior, not the person

Focus on the specific behaviors on hand that are causing the conflict and avoid personal attacks or accusations.

Set boundaries

Make it clear that you will not tolerate disrespectful or unprofessional behavior. This might involve setting boundaries around language, tone, or behavior during the conversation.

Seek mediation

If the conflict is escalating or cannot be resolved through direct communication, consider seeking mediation from a neutral third party. A mediator can facilitate the conversation and help the parties find a resolution.

Effective conflict management isn't just about resolving individual disputes. It is about creating a culture where open communication and respect are normal. As a leader, it is your job to create and instill this culture.

This can be done in multiple ways, including:

Encouraging open communication

Create a culture where team members feel comfortable expressing their opinions, even if they differ from the majority. Remember, someone doesn't have to be the majority to be correct. You should regularly solicit feedback and encourage open discussions where all opinions and ideas are welcome.

Addressing the conflict early

Never allow conflicts to fester. Address issues promptly and constructively before they escalate.

Setting clear expectations

Establish clear guidelines for respectful communication and conflict resolution. Make sure everyone understands the importance of professional behavior and the consequences of violating those expectations.

By cultivating this culture, you can be sure that team members will feel valued and heard, even when tensions begin to rise. By making sure your team members walk away from a conflict on a positive note, any frustrations or tension will not be carried over into the next conflict, whenever it may come about.

EXAMPLES

Let's look at an example in the workplace where these techniques can be employed to manage a conflict between two team members.

A development team is in the final stages of launching a new software product. The project has been intense, with long hours and high stakes. Tensions are running high.

In a meeting to finalize the launch plan, a miscommunication erupts into a heated argument between the lead developer and the product manager. The developer, James, accuses the product manager, Ashley, of changing the product specs without consulting the development team, which will cause delays. Ashley fires back that she sent out an email detailing the changes weeks ago and that everyone should have been aware already. The argument quickly escalates, with both teams taking sides.

Their manager, Rachel, steps in to de-escalate. She acknowledges the frustration and concern, but emphasizes that blaming each other won't resolve the issue. Their manager asks that everyone take a quick break and return to the conference room in ten minutes.

Once everyone has calmed down and returned to the conference room, Rachel facilitates the conversation. She starts by having James and Ashley share their perspectives using 'I' statements, focusing on their feelings and experiences rather than attacking each other.

Through active listening, the underlying issues become clear. James felt blindsided by the spec changes, which made him worry about reaching the launch deadline. Ashley thought she had communicated the changes clearly, but realized she could have confirmed that everyone was on the same page.

Rachel helps the team see that their shared interest is to successfully launch the product. They agree on a plan to clarify the specs, assess the impact of the changes, and create a contingency plan. Both

James and Ashley commit to improving their communication, with Ashley agreeing to confirm important updates in addition to emailing them, and James agreeing to make sure he double checks his email, in case he missed something.

Over the next few days, the team implements the plan. They are able to adjust the launch timeline slightly and add resources to absorb the impact of the spec changes. James and Ashley check in regularly, ensuring the new communication plan is working.

The launch ultimately happens successfully, although a little later than initially planned, but with the quality expected intact. The team reflects on what they have learned.

Miscommunication escalated the issue, but by addressing it openly and finding common ground, they were able to resolve the conflict and deliver the product.

LESSONS APPLIED

Give it time
Rachel didn't try to force a resolution in the heat of the moment. She gave the team space to cool down before addressing the issue.

Use 'I' statements
By focusing on their feelings and experiences, James and Ashley were able to express their concerns without blaming each other.

Active listening
Hearing each other's perspectives helped the team understand the underlying issues that were driving the conflict.

Focus on interests
Despite their disagreement, the shared interest in launching the product successfully provided a solid foundation for resolution.

Agree on a plan

The clear plan for moving forward helped prevent further misunderstandings.

Follow through

Checking in regularly ensures that the agreement held and adjustments could be made as needed.

By applying these conflict resolution strategies, this development company was able to navigate a potential derailment and successfully launch their product. The experience strengthened their collaboration and communication, making them better equipped to handle future challenges.

In this chapter we have explored techniques for handling difficult conversations, whether it be bringing up a team member's poor performance, or managing conflict within a team. We also went over the importance of cultivating a culture of open communication and respect, as well as an example of conflict management in action using some of the techniques shown in the chapter.

By implementing these strategies, you can transform difficult conversations from potential sources of tension into opportunities for growth and understanding.

CHAPTER 10

Digital Communication

The internet has changed everything. We expect to know everything instantly. If you don't understand digital communication, you're at a disadvantage.
-Bob Parsons

The evolution of communication technology has revolutionized the way we connect, share information, and lead. From the days of smoke signals and carrier pigeons to the advent of the telegraph, telephone and the internet, technology has progressively shortened the distance between people and accelerated the speed at which ideas travel. This relentless advancement has profoundly impacted the landscape of leadership communication, shaping how leaders interact with their teams, engage stakeholders, and navigate the complexities of the modern business world.

Before the digital age, leadership communication was largely confined to face-to-face interactions, letters, and occasional phone calls. These methods, while effective in their time, were inherently limited by geographical constraints and time required for information dissemination. The emergence of the internet and mobile devices fundamentally changed this paradigm, democratizing communication and enabling leaders to connect with their teams, partners, and customers in real-time, regardless of their physical location.

Digital advancement has led to the rise of numerous communication tools and platforms that have become indispensable for effective leadership communication. Email, instant messaging, video conferencing, and social media platforms have become primary channels for information sharing, collaboration, and relationship building. Leaders can now instantly communicate with their teams across time zones, conduct virtual meetings, share updates and announcements, and engage with employees on a more personal level.

However, this technological shift has also introduced new complexities and challenges for leaders. The constant influx of information through various channels can lead to information overload, making it difficult for individuals to discern critical information from unnecessary distractions. Additionally, the asynchronous nature of digital communication can lead to misinterpretation and misunderstandings, as subtle nuances of tone and intent can get lost in translation.

Navigating these complexities of digital communication requires leaders to cultivate a heightened awareness of their communication style, the potential pitfalls of digital platforms, and the importance of maintaining professionalism in online interactions. It is key for leaders to be mindful of the appropriate tone and language when communicating digitally, ensuring that their messages are clear, concise, and appropriate.

The rise of social media has also presented new opportunities and challenges for leadership communication. Leaders can leverage social media to build their personal brands, engage with employees, and foster a sense of community within their organizations. However, the public nature of social media requires leaders to be cautious about their online presence, and be mindful of the potential for misinterpretations and the importance of maintaining a professional image.

The influence of technology on leadership communication is not limited to communication tools and platforms. The advent of artificial intelligence (AI) and machine learning is further transforming the way leaders communicate and manage information. AI-powered tools can now automate routine tasks, analyze large datasets to identify trends and insights, and even provide personalized recommendations for improving communication strategies.

In essence, the evolution of communication technology has both empowered and complicated the task of effective leadership communication. Leaders must embrace the opportunities presented by these advancements while remaining mindful of the potential pitfalls and ensuring that their communication remains authentic, engaging and human-centered. The future of leadership communication is likely to be characterized by an even greater integration of technology, necessitating a proactive and adaptable approach from leaders. Embracing this dynamic landscape requires continuous learning, a willingness to experiment with new tools and strategies, and a commitment to upholding a culture of open and effective communication.

EMAIL

This tool has remained a cornerstone of business communication since its inception. Email's ability to share information and remain formal in tone makes it ideal for various professional exchanges. Here are ways in which leaders can utilize email for maximum impact:

Craft a clear and concise message

The first step to effective email communication is writing clearly and concisely. No one wants to open their email and read an entire essay. Keep paragraphs short and use bullet points or numbered lists for clarity when presenting multiple points. For any long form communication, video conferencing or in-person meetings are more effective.

Your email should be easy to understand, free of jargon and slang, and focused on the most important information. Always begin with a strong, relevant subject line that accurately reflects the information within. Avoid being vague in the subject line as well. For instance, instead of "Meeting Notes," you should use "Sales Meeting Notes-September 26th" or a variation thereof. This makes the email easier to identify and find when needed.

Target your audience

It is important to remember that email is not one-size-fits-all. Tailor your message to your audience. Consider their role, level of understanding and expectations. For example, a junior team member may require more comprehensive and detailed instructions than a senior team member.

Proofread carefully

A mistake often made in emails are grammatical errors and typos. Always proofread your email thoroughly before hitting send; a well-written email says a lot about your professionalism and attention to detail.

Use proper etiquette

Appropriate email etiquette is crucial for maintaining a professional image. Always use a professional greeting and closing. Don't get too caught up in choosing the perfect greeting and closing, it's the information contained within the email that people care about. As long as the greeting and closing is professional, and the message is clear and concise, you have set the stage for a positive and impactful exchange.

Consider time zones

If communicating with colleagues in different parts of the world, be mindful of their working hours. Sending an email late at night in their time zone indicates a lack of consideration and awareness. Instead, schedule the email to be sent at a time convenient for them.

Utilize email features

Most email platforms offer features like calendar invites, task management tools, and scheduled sending. These tools are there to maximize production and make your life easier.

Maintain professionalism

Email communication is a permanent record, so it is necessary to be mindful of your words and maintain a professional tone throughout. Avoid using slang and overly informal language.

Follow up

After sending an email, follow up if necessary. This ensures that your message has been received and that you are receptive to inquiries.

ADDITIONAL TIPS FOR CRAFTING A PROFESSIONAL EMAIL

The first few lines

1. Include the topic and purpose of the email in the subject line
2. Indicate urgency in the subject line, if needed
3. In the first line (after the greeting) state your request
4. Deliver the most important information in the first few lines, so that it does not get lost in the email
5. Specify the response deadline

6.   Only change the subject line if there was an error (typo, incorrect date, etc.)

Format and layout

1.   In addition to keeping the email itself short, keep each paragraph concise to maintain the reader's attention
2.   Put any questions, actionable items, and decisions to be made in their own lines
3.   Label questions, actionable items, and decisions for increased clarity
4.   Repeat questions from colleague's emails when answering them in yours

Group emails, chains, and forwarding

1.   If you add someone to an email chain, explain why they were added–both to the person added and the group
2.   The same should be done if someone is removed from an email chain
3.   Add a summary of key points when forwarding an email chain–tools like Chat GPT, Google Gemini, or any other AI LLM (large language model) will be capable of doing this for you
4.   Don't drift the topic in an email chain, either make sure the group stays on track, or start a new email chain for a different topic
5.   If a conversation carries on outside of the email chain (like in a video call or in-person) return to the email chain and summarize the key points

VIDEO CONFERENCING

Video conferencing has become an essential tool for remote collaboration and communication. According to the Bureau of Labor Statistics, one in five employees in the United States worked remotely as of 2023 [25]. With that number climbing every year, the importance of remote meetings is ever-growing. Here is how leaders can master video conferencing:

Invest in quality equipment

Clear audio and video are paramount for an effective video conference. Investing in a high-quality webcam and microphone for optimal sound and image quality if your computer's built in camera and microphone are not up to par. You will also need to make sure your home WiFi network has a strong connection to mitigate buffering on both your end and your colleague's end. Nothing is more frustrating during a video conference than not being able to hear what is being said because the video connection is breaking up constantly.

Preparation is key

Treat a video conference no differently than a face-to-face meeting. Plan your agenda, prepare your materials, and ensure you are familiar with your video conferencing platform and any relevant features you will need to use during the call (think screen-sharing, built-in chat box, breakout rooms, and call recording are all useful tools to utilize).

Dress professionally

Just as you would for an in-person meeting, dress professionally for video conferences as well. This maintains professionalism and projects a positive image.

Record the session if necessary

Recording the session can be useful for a couple reasons. It can be used for future reference, and can be watched at a later time by anyone unable to attend the meeting live. To do this, ensure you have the consent from the participants before starting the recording.

Actively engage

Video conferencing requires active participation. Asking questions, offering a ppropriate f eedback, a nd a ffirmations are all great ways to show you are engaged with the team member that is speaking.

Mute yourself when not speaking

Muting your microphone when you are not speaking minimizes background noise and distractions for others in the call. Just remember to unmute yourself before speaking.

Follow up after the meeting

Just as you would after a traditional meeting, send a summary of key points and any agreed-upon actions so that there is a written record of the important points of the meeting.

SOCIAL MEDIA

Next, we will look at social media. Social media has become a powerful tool for leaders to connect with their teams, stakeholders, and consumers. Platforms like LinkedIn, Instagram, and Facebook provide opportunities to share company news, build relationships and foster a sense of community. However, using social media effectively requires careful planning and execution. Here are the ways you can get the most of out this invaluable tool:

Define your purpose

Before launching into social media, you must first d efine your goals. What do you hope to achieve with your online presence? Are you aiming to build brand awareness, share industry insights, or engage directly with your audience?

Choose the right platforms

Not all social media platforms are created equal. Consider your target audience and choose platforms that best suit your objectives. For example, LinkedIn is the ideal platform for professional networking, whereas Instagram is best suited for building brand awareness due to the high volume of users.

Create engaging content

Your social media content should be valuable, informative, and most importantly, engaging. Using a healthy mix of text, images, and videos throughout your timeline to keep engagement high.

Consistency is key

Consistency is paramount to building a strong social media presence. Post regularly, even if it is just once or twice a week, to keep your followers engaged and informed.

Be authentic

Share genuine insights, experiences, and perspectives that are a reflection of yourself, or your company's culture and values. By failing to be authentic, your followers will fail to engage with your content as it may seem forced and uninspired.

Respond to your audience

Engage with followers by responding to comments, questions and messages promptly. This shows that you value their input and are actively listening to their feedback.

Monitor your analytics

Track your social media analytics to understand what content resonates with your audience. This will help you evolve your strategy, and create better content that resonates with your followers.

Stay updated

The social media landscape is constantly evolving. Stay up-to-date on new platforms, features, and best practices to optimize your strategy and stay ahead of the curve.

In today's digitally driven world, mastering digital communication is essential for leaders. By understanding the nuances of email, video conferencing, and social media, leaders can connect with their teams, engage with stakeholders, and build strong relationships in the digital age. With a strategic approach and mindful execution, these tools can become powerful assets for leading effectively and achieving success in a world where communication is more critical than ever.

CHAPTER 11

Building Relationships
and Networks

Personal relationships are the fertile soil from which all
advancement, all success, all achievement in real life grows.
-Ben Stein

For far too many people, networking is simply about collecting business cards and connecting with people on LinkedIn. Unfortunately, if they make no effort to actively use these connections, they have done nothing but waste their own time. Networking is a strategic investment in your leadership journey and career trajectory. While often conflated, networking and relationship building are distinct yet intertwined processes. Networking focuses on expanding your professional connections and creating a vast web of contacts across various industries and sectors. It's about strategically identifying and engaging with individuals who can offer valuable insights, support, or opportunities.

On the other hand, relationship building is a more profound, sustained endeavor focused on cultivating genuine connections based on mutual trust, respect, and shared interests. It relies on fostering strong, long-term relationships with individuals who can become trusted advisors, collaborators, or even mentors. Effective leadership requires a strong network that provides access to a wealth of resources and perspectives and meaningful relationships that provide the foundation for sustained collaboration and mutual support. The most successful leaders understand this delicate balance, leveraging both networking and relationship-building to enhance their effectiveness as leaders and achieve their goals. They know genuine connections are the bedrock of impactful leadership, and networking is a gateway to forging these critical relationships.

BUILDING YOUR NETWORK

Building a robust and effective network requires a proactive and strategic approach. Attending industry events or connecting with people on social media is not enough. Leaders must develop a thoughtful strategy to identify key individuals whose expertise or experience aligns with their professional goals. This involves conducting thorough research, utilizing online resources like LinkedIn and professional organizations, and leveraging existing connections to identify potential contacts. Consider the scenario of a financial advisor looking to expand their client base. Instead of randomly approaching individuals, they might research high-net-worth people in their community, identifying their interests and professional networks. The advisor can tailor their approach by understanding their needs and aspirations, building rapport, and demonstrating a genuine interest in providing valuable financial solutions. This targeted approach maximizes the effectiveness of their networking efforts, yielding more meaningful connections and opportunities.

Once key individuals are identified, initiating contact and building rapport is next. This involves more than simply exchanging pleasantries. It requires real, tangible engagement and active listening. Building trust takes time and effort, requiring consistent communication and demonstrable reliability. Consider the impact of a simple gesture like sending a personalized note following a networking event, thanking the person for their time, and reiterating a shared point of conversation. This small action demonstrates attentiveness and genuine interest, significantly enhancing the chances of fostering a long-term relationship. Authenticity is essential; individuals can quickly discern insincerity, undermining efforts to build trust and rapport.

The most effective networks are not solely about extracting value, instead they are built on reciprocity and mutual benefit principles. Leaders who approach networking with a selfish mindset, focused solely on their gain, are unlikely to cultivate strong relationships. Think about it from the other person's perspective; why would you spend your precious time on someone who only extracts benefits for themselves if you are not getting anything in return? In contrast, leaders who embrace a collaborative spirit, offering support and assistance to others, create a virtuous cycle of mutual benefit and gain. This may involve providing referrals, sharing valuable insights, or assisting colleagues or contacts. Consider the impact of a leader who consistently advocates for the success of their team members, helping them secure promotions or recognition. This generous approach builds strong relationships within the team and strengthens their reputation as a supportive and collaborative leader.

NETWORKING IN ACTION

Now, let's examine the contrasting experiences of two individuals aspiring to leadership roles within their organizations. On one side, we have Will. Will attends networking events focusing on exchanging business cards to expand his contact list and his connections on LinkedIn. However, he lacks genuine interest in the people he meets, focusing instead on extracting information or opportunities without reciprocal engagement. His interactions are superficial and transactional, leaving little to no lasting impact.

In stark contrast, Mason approaches these networking events with a completely different mindset. He is here for the *people*, not just the business cards. He strategically identifies individuals whose expertise or experience aligns with his career goals and aspirations. He invests time learning about other people's backgrounds and goals, engaging in thoughtful conversation, and actively listening to their perspectives. He offers support when he can, demonstrating his genuine interest in their success. As a result, Mason cultivates strong relationships with key individuals who become sources of advice, support, and mentorship, providing him with valuable opportunities for professional advancement. His success is a testament to the power of genuine engagement and the long-term benefits of prioritizing relationship-building over mere network expansion.

MAINTAINING RELATIONSHIPS

Maintaining and nurturing the professional relationships you've cultivated requires consistent effort and a thoughtful approach. As we've been through, collecting business cards is not enough; you must actively invest your time into these relationships to ensure they remain valuable assets. Think of your network as an expansive and vast garden–it requires consistent effort to flourish. However, you get a vast array of fresh fruits and vegetables. Neglect will lead to wilting connections and missed opportunities. Proactive communication, consistent engagement, and genuine interest are paramount.

Remember those informational interviews you conducted while building your network? Reciprocity is key; now it's time to offer your assistance. Do contacts need advice in your area of expertise?

Are there opportunities you can introduce them to? Could you provide a helpful recommendation or connect them with someone who could benefit from their work? Actively seeking ways to support your network demonstrates your commitment to the relationship and fosters a sense of mutual benefit. This reciprocity strengthens the bonds and ensures the longevity of your connections.

Regular communication is crucial, but the *quality* of the communication matters more. Avoid generic, mass-produced emails or messages. Anyone can spot generic messages in an instant. Personalization is crucial. Tailor your communication to the individual, referencing specific projects, achievements, or conversations you've previously shared. This demonstrates that you remember and value the details of your interactions, showing genuine interest in their journey.

In addition to email, consider utilizing other methods of communication to enhance your relationships. A brief phone call can be more personal and engaging than an email, allowing for a deeper connection and a more natural conversation. But be aware that not everyone is receptive to phone calls in the modern age. Many prefer emails or even a message on LinkedIn instead. You must utilize the lessons in the second chapter to understand your audience.

Consider an occasional lunch meeting or a coffee together for closer contact. This can be incredibly valuable for building rapport and maintaining a strong connection. One study from *Harvard Business Review* found that 95% of professionals believed that face-to-face meetings cultivated stronger long-term relationships [26]. Plus, no one is going to turn down a free lunch.

Remember that these are not networking events. They are opportunities to learn about each other's lives beyond the workplace and to foster trust and understanding.

Consider leveraging technology to enhance communication and maintain relationships. LinkedIn is invaluable for staying updated on your contacts' professional achievements. Engaging with their posts, creating meaningful comments, and sharing relevant articles can reinforce your connection. Utilizing professional networking platforms is a way to expand your network and nurture existing ones.

You must also remember the importance of celebrating your contacts' achievements. Whether it's a promotion, an award, or the successful completion of a significant p roject, a cknowledging their success reinforces your appreciation and strengthens the relationship. A sincere congratulatory message, a public endorsement on a professional networking site, or a personal note can go a long way in showing your support. This demonstrates that you value their contribution and remain attentive to their progress. Furthermore, offering support during challenging times can also strengthen the bond. If a contact faces a setback, offering encouragement and assistance can be invaluable, building trust and loyalty.

Another essential aspect of maintaining professional relationships (generally) is being reliable and responsive. If you commit to something, follow through. If you promise information or assistance, do it promptly and thoroughly. Reliability builds trust and demonstrates your professionalism. Conversely, being unresponsive or unreliable can severely damage the relationship. Promptness and professionalism are essential for keeping strong professional ties.

However, as mentioned earlier, maintaining relationships is a two-way street. You should be prepared to disengage from relationships that are no longer mutually b eneficial r elationships. This doesn't mean abandoning or ghosting people. It means recognizing that priorities and circumstances change and refocusing your efforts on the most valuable connections is okay. Having a small, highly engaged network is better than a large, passive one. Periodically review your network and assess which relationships require more attention and which have naturally run their course. Remember that networking is an ongoing process of cultivation and refinement.

Cultivating strong and lasting professional relationships demands a thoughtful, strategic, and consistent approach. It's a continuous journey of engagement, reciprocity, and genuine support, requiring proactive communication and a willingness to invest time and energy. By embracing this ongoing process, you transform your network from a mere collection of contacts into a powerful asset, driving your career forward and enhancing your overall professional success. The strength of your professional network directly correlates to your ability to navigate challenges, seize opportunities, and achieve your professional goals. The investment in these relationships is an investment in your future. It's not just about quantity but the quality and depth of the connections you cultivate. And that quality is what sets the truly successful networkers apart. It is a dynamic and evolving system that requires constant attention and mindful cultivation.

Part III: Advanced Leadership Communication

CHAPTER 12

Negotiation and Persuasion

Let us never negotiate out of fear. But let us never fear to negotiate.
-John F. Kennedy

It is commonly believed that negotiation is a battle of wills–that is, the person who concedes the most in the negotiation is the *loser*. Yet, despite this commonly perceived notion, effective negotiation is far more than that; it's a sophisticated dance of strategy, empathy, and persuasive communication. It's about achieving mutually beneficial outcomes, not just winning at all costs. This understanding forms the bedrock of successful negotiations, transforming them from heart racing confrontations into collaborative problem-solving sessions.

While these pages are about leadership communication in business, we have to also understand that negotiation is undeniably an integral part of communication in life itself, whether it's haggling over the price of a car, or resolving conflict within a recreational basketball team. The ability to negotiate effectively is a valuable skill that can significantly impact personal as well as professional success. Mastering the art of negotiation involves understanding the dynamics at play, carefully preparing for the process, and employing effective communication strategies.

UNDERSTANDING NEGOTIATION DYNAMICS: A DANCE OF INTERESTS

Negotiation is essentially a dance of interests. It involves identifying common ground, addressing conflicting interests, and finding mutually acceptable solutions. Both parties come to the table with their own needs, desires, and objectives. These interests may be diverse, ranging from tangible factors like price and delivery terms to intangible ones like reputation and future relationships. Identifying and understanding these dynamics is crucial for navigating the negotiation process successfully.

Effective negotiation requires a deep understanding of both your own interests and those of the other party. It involves asking insightful questions, actively listening to responses, and sharing relevant information to facilitate productive dialogue. By doing so, you can uncover creative solutions that satisfy both parties' core interests. This collaborative approach often leads to more durable agreements and stronger relationships compared to competitive negotiation tactics focused solely on 'winning.'

A crucial aspect of interest-based negotiation is separating interests from positions. Positions are specific, often inflexible proposals put forth by a party. Interests, on the other hand, are the underlying needs, desires, or concerns that led to those positions. By exploring the interests behind a position, negotiators develop innovative options that better address both parties' needs. For instance, in a contract negotiation, one party might take the position that they cannot pay more than $X per unit. However, their underlying interest could be a concern about profitability or budget constraints. If the other party can provide increased value through extended warranties, premium service, or bulk discount, they may be able to structure a deal that meets the first party's profitability interest while still achieving their own pricing objectives.

Negotiation is not a zero-sum game, where one side's gain equals the other's loss. With a principled, interest based approach, negotiators can often create value and reach agreements that leave both parties better off than their initial positions. This requires open-mindedness, creativity, and a willingness to collaborate. By focusing on interests, separating them from positions, and exploring mutually beneficial options, negotiators can turn the negotiation 'dance' into a rewarding and productive process for all involved.

PREPARING FOR NEGOTIATION

A cornerstone of successful negotiation, effective preparation involves a comprehensive understanding of the subject matter, the other party's interests, and your own goals and priorities. You also need to anticipate potential challenges and prepare counterarguments.

There are six steps to negotiation preparation. In order, they are as follows:

1. Research the subject matter
Gain in-depth knowledge of the negotiation topic. This includes understanding the current market, recent news and developments, and any relevant facts or figures. The more informed you are, the stronger your position will be.

2. Analyze the counterpart
You must be able to see things from the other party's perspective. What are their needs, desires, goals, and limitations? What pressures are they under, and how might this impact the negotiation? The bet-

ter you understand their point of view, the more effectively you can address their concerns and find mutually beneficial solutions.

3. Define your objectives

Clearly articulate your goals for the negotiation. What is your ideal outcome, and what is your minimum position? Prioritize your objectives, and distinguish the difference between needs and wants. This will provide a roadmap for your negotiation strategy.

4. Anticipate obstacles

Think about potential roadblocks and disagreements. What objections might the other party raise, and how can you counter these effectively? Prepare persuasive arguments and creative solutions in advance. The ability to address concerns in a compelling way will strengthen your negotiating power.

5. Rehearse different scenarios

Consider various negotiation scenarios, from the most favorable to the most challenging. Visualize how you will respond to different tactics or demands from the other party. This mental rehearsal will enhance your confidence and agility during the actual negotiation.

6. Select the right negotiation style

Choose a negotiation approach that aligns with the situation and your relationship with your counterpart. This could involve competitive tactics, collaborative problem solving, or a more accommodating approach. The key is to remain flexible and adapt your style as the negotiation unfolds.

In addition to these six steps of negotiation preparation, you also need to create a **B**est **A**lternative **T**o a **N**egotiated **A**greement (BATNA) [27]. This idea may have been developed back in 1981, but the idea has been a staple of negotiating since its inception. A BATNA represents your fallback position, the best alternative if the current negotiation fails. Knowing your BATNA empowers you to set realistic expectations and establish a firm negotiation stance. If the negotiation doesn't yield a favorable outcome, you have a clear alternative to fall back on, preventing you from settling for something less than satisfactory.

For instance, imagine that you are negotiating a job offer from a different employer. Your BATNA might be another job offer entirely, or it could be your current salary with your current employer. Having a solid BATNA gives you the confidence to walk away from a negotiation if the terms aren't beneficial to you. It also provides a reference point during the negotiation, helping you determine whether the proposed terms are better than your alternatives.

KEY ELEMENTS

Now that we have looked at how to prepare for a successful negotiation, let's now shift our focus to the key elements of a successful negotiation;

Active listening

You're starting to see a pattern, aren't you? Active listening is a critical theme throughout the lessons outlined in these pages. It is one of the strongest skills a leader can have, and is imperative to possess in all walks of life, whether professional or personal. But in the scope of negotiation, active listening allows you to fully understand the other party's perspective and interests. It involves paying close attention, asking clarifying questions, and summarizing the other party's points to ensure understanding. Knowing what the other party wants out of the negotiation helps you better find an applicable solution that will be a win for both parties involved. Active listening demonstrates respect and builds trust, creating a more conducive environment for finding mutually acceptable solutions. It also helps identify potential areas of compromise and find creative solutions that address the needs of both sides of the negotiation.

Creative problem solving

Look for innovative solutions that address the needs of all parties involved. Think outside the box to find solutions that go beyond traditional bargaining approaches.

Aim for win-win outcomes

The best outcomes are the ones where both parties walk out the door in a better situation than they walked in with. This builds a relationship between both parties and opens the door for more pragmatic negotiations in the future.

Be patient and persistent

Negotiations can often require a great deal of time to reach a resolution acceptable for both parties. Stay calm, composed, and focused on your objectives. Avoid making impulsive concessions or decisions based on pressure or emotion.

Be willing to compromise

While not ideal, a willingness to compromise may be the only way to reach an agreement that is better than the alternative (walking away empty-handed). Be prepared to make concessions, but only on issues that are less important to you.

Be willing to walk away

This is only a last resort, and is only applicable if compromising is worse than your BATNA you created earlier. You must know your limits and be prepared to end the negotiation if the terms are unfavorable. A willingness to walk away demonstrates confidence in your position and can prompt the other party to make concessions. Think of a car salesman for example. While car salesmen get paid a yearly salary, they also get a commission for every car they sell. That increases the desire to sell the car, and makes selling the vehicle at a lower price now, better than not selling the car at all. When a potential customer and a salesman cannot agree on a price, walking away can prompt the salesman to make one final stride to sell the vehicle, and may get you a more favorable price. While this should be your last resort in a negotiation, it can be a useful tool to get better terms.

With these ideas in mind, you are now ready to ace the negotiation process. From preparation, creating a BATNA, to strategies for success, you now possess all the tools you need to navigate negotiations with confidence and achieve your goals. Remember that negotiation is a skill that improves with practice, so seek out opportunities to hone your abilities. Over time, you will become a more effective and influential negotiator, capable of driving successful outcomes in all aspects of your personal and professional life.

CHAPTER 13

Crisis Communication

The ultimate measure of a man is not where he stands in the moments of comfort, but where he stands at times of challenge and controversy.
-Martin Luther King Jr.

C risis can strike any business unexpectedly. These difficult situations threaten a company's reputation, financial stability, and can even threaten its very survival. These sudden events can range from cyber attacks and natural disasters to product recalls and scandals.

Navigating a crisis effectively is vital for any leader in order to mitigate damage, restore trust, and keep the company's reputation from collapsing. By the successful development and implementation of a strategic crisis communication plan, leaders can minimize the negative impact of the crisis and return stronger than before.

This chapter will explore the four stages of crisis communication, as well as the key principles of navigating a crisis effectively. We will also have case studies outlining the importance of these key principles.

By understanding the best practices of crisis communication, leaders can be better prepared to face adversity if/when it hits, and emerge from it with their organization's reputation intact.

FOUR KEY STAGES OF CRISIS COMMUNICATION

First, let us look at the four key stages of crisis communication. They are as follows:

1. Preparation

Given the unforeseen nature of a crisis, staying prepared and having a plan in place can help keep your business ahead of uncertainty. The first step in preparation is the development of a crisis communication plan. This will include identifying potential risks and vulnerabilities that the organization could face. For example, if you run an oil company, a potential crisis would be an oil spill, or for a car company, it would be a mass recall to fix a dangerous safety issue. Sometimes, though, identifying a potential risk may be a bit harder. If you are a non-profit organization, for example, you may have some difficulty finding a specific crisis your organization may face. In this case, you can take a more generalized approach of the following steps.

The next step is a critical one; the crisis management team. This will be the group of people, composed of key stakeholders and decision makers, that will lead the organization through rough waters, and hopefully, as unscathed as possible. Making sure the roles and responsibilities of each member of the crisis management team is essential to ensuring seamless communication and action during the crisis. The crisis management team roles and responsibilities will vary from organization to organization, and should be created based upon the size and needs of the company. One role that will not change is the spokesperson of the crisis management team. This is normally the head of the organization, but sometimes this role can also be fulfilled by the Chief Communications Officer.

Next, the organization should create a holding statement. This is a pre-approved message or template which will allow the company to express empathy, but not admit fault as it investigates the crisis.

Holding statements can be for something as small as a network outage, b ut the importance is the same regardless–to let the public know that the organization is aware, empathetic towards the issue, and is working on solving the problem and taking corrective action. Holding statements should always include the date and time, location of the incident, and only details and information that have been *confirmed*. A holding statement should never include rumors or speculation, nor should it shift the blame to another person/entity/company.

The final step to preparation is to establish clear communication channels. During a crisis, rumors and speculation can spread like wildfire, and can further damage a company's reputation if the rumors are not put to rest immediately. Organizations should leverage multiple communication channels, including social media, digital publications, the company's website, and traditional forms of media in order to reach a large audience and quell any rumors and outcry. In today's day and age, social media and digital publications are the most effective as they can reach a large audience in a short amount of time.

2. Response

Now it's time to put your preparation plan into effect. A swift and effective response is paramount when faced with a crisis, and the preparation plan serves as a guide to navigate this tricky situation. All members of the crisis management team should be notified and ready to get to work managing the crisis response.

The first few hours are critical in crisis management, and set the tone for the entire response. As a leader, it is up to you to lead your team through this. The pre-approved holding statements should be disseminated through the established communication channels. Transparency is key here, as updates should be provided as they become available and are confirmed.

The designated spokesperson plays a pivotal role during the response phase. This individual serves as the face and voice of the organization, relaying messages to the public, media, and stakeholders. Honesty and empathy are very important, as inaccurate information and/or lack of empathy can exacerbate the situation.

Decisive action is another hallmark of an effective crisis response. The organization must take swift action to address the crisis, whether it be a product recall, issuing refunds for a faulty/rushed product, or disciplining those involved in misconduct cases. Failure to take immediate action on these issues deteriorates trust in the organization, and is harmful to the reputation of the company. Transparent and empathetic communication helps rebuild trust and demonstrates accountability.

Throughout the response phase, continual monitoring and assessment are vital. The crisis management team should stay aware of all new developments, and should adjust the response strategy as needed.

3. Recovery

The main goal of the recovery phase is to not only rebuild trust, but the organization's reputation. This may involve donating money to a related charitable cause, or it may be as simple as assuring the public the issue will not happen again (it all depends on the severity of the crisis, and it is up to leadership to make the call of what corrective actions are appropriate to rebuild the trust and the reputation of the company).

4. Learning

In the final stage, a post crisis analysis must be conducted to identify lessons learned and areas that need to be improved upon in the crisis communication plan. This stage cannot be overlooked. History is our greatest teacher, and through it, we have many valuable lessons to be learned. The origin of the issue must be addressed to prevent the crisis from happening again, and stakeholders should be kept in the loop of all preventative measures taken as a result of this phase.

The strengths and weaknesses of the crisis management team must also be addressed. What worked? What didn't? How did the public respond to the response phase? The recovery phase? Any shortcomings must be identified and fixed to maximize the effectiveness of the crisis management team going forward.

Now that we know the four phases of crisis management, let's look at the ten key principles 0f navigating a crisis effectively.

10 KEY PRINCIPLES TO NAVIGATING A CRISIS EFFECTIVELY

1. Decisiveness

Decisive leadership provides clear direction, helping teams focus their efforts despite the chaos. Without clear and actionable direction, people may feel paralyzed or adrift as the chaos unfolds. In a crisis, every minute counts. Decisive leaders drive swift action, preventing further damage or capitalizing on opportunities before they slip away. When leaders make quick, confident decisions, it instills trust in their teams. People are more likely to rally behind a confident leader who knows what they are doing. Decisiveness cuts through ambiguity. It forces leaders to prioritize what is truly important and make tough calls, even in the face of uncertainty.

2. Transparency

Open communication builds trust with employees, stakeholders, and the public. When leaders share information freely, it demonstrates honesty and respect. This trust is critical for navigating a crisis. By providing clear, factual updates, leaders can ensure everyone has a consistent understanding of the situation. Transparency also fosters collaboration. When teams understand the full context of what is happening, they can contribute more meaningfully to find solutions.

Transparency also helps build resilience. Stakeholders are better equipped to weather the crisis when they understand what is happening and how they can contribute. Regular updates are key, even if there is no major news. Silence creates a vacuum that rumors often fill. Share what you know, what you are doing, and what you are still figuring out. Acknowledge the challenges and difficulties, but also highlight efforts and progress. Ensure messaging is consistent across all channels.

Remember, transparency is more than just sharing information, it is about creating an open, honest culture where employees and stakeholders feel valued and empowered. While it may be challenging in the heat of a crisis, the benefits in terms of trust, collaboration, and resilience make it well worth the effort.

3. Empathy

Empathy allows leaders to understand and share the feelings of those affected by the crisis. When leaders demonstrate compassion, it helps individuals feel seen and validated. This acknowledgement of their emotional experience is crucial for building trust and resilience. Empathetic leaders create a safe space where people feel comfortable expressing their fears, anxieties, and concerns. This openness can lead to more honest communication and collaboration. Empathy also fosters a sense of community. When leaders show that they care about the well being of not only those affected, but team members and stakeholders as well, it strengthens the bonds and encourages people to support one another. In a crisis, this sense of unity is vital for navigating the challenges ahead.

Empathy is all about perspective. Try to imagine how the crisis is impacting others. Put yourself in their shoes and consider their unique challenges and fears. This can help leaders make more compassionate decisions. Make an effort to understand the experiences of frontline staff, customers, and the broader community. Seek out diverse perspectives to gain a more well-rounded understanding of what is happening. Empathy is a skill that can be developed with practice. The more you focus on building your empathetic skills, the more naturally it will become part of your leadership style. While empathy may seem like a "soft" skill, its impact on trust, collaboration, and resilience makes it a critical component of effective crisis leadership.

4. Clarity

Clear communication is the bedrock of effective crisis management. Don't get it confused with transparency, while transparency is about creating a culture of honesty and openness, clarity is about making sure your words don't get tangled, whether between communication channels or by the press. Clarity eliminates any potential confusion and ensures everyone is on the same page enabling swift action, as team members and stakeholders fully understand what is expected of them.

Decisiveness promotes clarity. Swift, confident decisions provide direction, even in the face of uncertainty. Leaders should be comfortable making tough calls, and explaining the reasoning behind them in a clear and concise manner. Clarity is about more than just communicating information; it is about creating a sense of focus and direction amidst the chaos of it all.

5. Collaboration

The ability to collaborate effectively allows leaders to tap into the collective wisdom and expertise of their teams. In a crisis, no one person has every answer, but by bringing together diverse perspectives, leaders can develop more innovative and effective solutions. Collaboration also encourages active participation, engaging people in the problem solving process. This in turn leads to greater ownership and motivation, as individuals feel that their contributions are valued. Collaboration also helps build trust. When leaders involve others in decision making, it demonstrates respect for their input and ideas. This can strengthen relationships and foster a sense of unity, which is critical for navigating the challenges of a crisis. It is important to understand that collaboration extends beyond the leadership team. Engaging frontline staff, customers, and the broader community to gain a more well-rounded understanding of the situation. These stakeholders often have valuable insights from their unique vantage points.

Open communication is the foundation of collaboration. Leaders should create a safe space where people feel comfortable sharing their ideas and concerns. Give your full attention to others and make sure that they feel heard is imperative. Ask open-ended questions to encourage collaboration, rather than merely seeking validation for your own ideas. Be transparent about goals, challenges, and progress, keeping everyone informed. Recognize and reward collaborative behavior, highlighting when people work well together. Keep in mind that collaboration requires a degree of vulnerability. Leaders must be comfortable admitting what they don't know and seeking help from others. This can be challenging, especially in the high-pressure context of a crisis. However, the benefits of creativity, engagement, and trust make collaboration a principle well worth embracing.

As a collaborative leader, you must provide the necessary resources and autonomy, giving peop;e the space to contribute their best work. Offer guidance rather than micromanaging, and trust in the abilities of your team (what worth is a leader who doesn't have faith in their own team?). Celebrate successes and learn from failures together, using challenges as opportunities for growth. Collaboration is about more than just working together–it's about creating a culture where diverse perspectives are valued and everyone has a stake in finding solutions. By fostering collaboration, leaders can build a resilient organization that is better equipped to weather the storms of a crisis.

6. Adaptability

During a crisis, leaders need to respond with agility and flexibility. During a crisis, the situation is often fluid, with new information and challenges emerging at a rapid pace. Adaptive leaders don't get flustered by these shifts; instead, they adjust plans as necessary, staying focused on the ultimate goal. This ability to pivot helps mitigate further damage and capitalize on opportunities as they arise. Adaptability requires a growth mindset, as leaders should embrace challenges as learning experiences, rather than threats to their ego. This openness to growth enables them to innovate solutions and navigate uncharted territory. Adaptive leaders empower their teams to make decisions. By providing a framework rather than rigid instructions, they give people the autonomy to respond to changing circumstances. This not only speeds up response times but also develops the problem solving skills of the team.

In a crisis, you must continually assess what is working and what is not, making adjustments based on feedback and new insights as they are made available. You can't be wedded to a particular plan if it is no longer serving the situation. The ability to let go of ineffective strategies is a hallmark of adaptive leadership. Stay open to new ideas and be willing to experiment. While not all experiments will be successful, they provide valuable learning regardless. Celebrate the efforts, not just the outcomes. Recognize the creativity and resilience of your team as they navigate the challenges of adapting to a crisis.

Adaptability is about more than just surviving a crisis— it's about emerging stronger on the other side. By embracing change and continually adapting, leaders can turn challenges into opportunities for growth and innovation. While adaptability can be demanding at first, the more leaders practice, the more it becomes second nature, enabling you to lead with confidence and agility, even in the most turbulent of times.

7. Accountability

Accountability starts with taking ownership of actions and their consequences. When leaders admit their mistakes and accept responsibility, it demonstrates integrity and builds trust. Trying to shift the blame or making excuses erodes credibility and exacerbates a crisis. Accountable leaders are transparent about challenges and failures, providing honest explanations rather than glossing over issues. This openness shows a commitment to learning and improvement. Hold yourself and others to high standards. Set clear expectations for behavior and performance, ensuring that everyone understands their role in navigating the crisis. Consistently enforce consequences for falling short, but also be fair and compassionate. Addressing misconduct or incompetence swiftly and decisively is crucial for maintaining trust.

When mistakes occur, conduct a thorough review to identify lessons learned. Implement changes to prevent similar issues in the future, demonstrating a commitment to growth and improvement. Lead by example. Demonstrate the same level of accountability you expect from others. Admit when you don't have the answers and involve others in finding the solutions. Show vulnerability and a willingness to learn, as this fosters a culture of accountability within your organization.

8. Optics

Optics refers to how your words and actions are perceived by others. In a crisis, every move will be scrutinized. Decisions and actions that are fair, compassionate, and transparent build trust, while those that appear self-serving or callous can erode confidence. Leaders need to consider how their words and actions will be perceived by employees, customers, shareholders, the media, and broader public. While it is impossible to satisfy everyone, demonstrating empathy and a commitment to doing what is right goes a long way in managing optics.

Imagine a scenario where a large corporation has been facing financial challenges, and announces a significant round of layoffs. This would be an extremely ill-advised time for the CEO to post an image online of their new Ferrari, for example. The optics of the CEO publicly sharing their expensive new purchase online is not in itself a bad thing, but the timing of posting it while mass layoffs are happening and thousands of employees are unsure how they will pay their rent next month is what makes the post tone-deaf and insensitive.

9. Learning

History is our greatest teacher, and mistakes are an asset to become better. Learning is a key of crisis management because it allows leaders to gain insights from the crisis and apply those lessons to future challenges. Rather than simply reacting to the immediate situation, leaders that learn and adapt seek to understand what worked well and what didn't, and how they can improve their response moving forward. This involves conducting thorough debriefs and after-action reviews once the crisis has passed. Gather feedback from stakeholders, employees, customers, and partners. Ask open-ended questions to encourage honest input, such as "What resources or support did you wish you had during the crisis, and how can we provide those in the future?" and "Describe a moment when you felt particularly supported or unsupported during the crisis? What contributed to that feeling?" Analyze the feedback and identify key themes and areas for improvement.

Once these are identified, now you need to implement changes based on what you have learned. This demonstrates a commitment to growth and improvement, and makes you and your organization better prepared when faced with more challenges down the road. This includes developing new strategies, updating protocols, and providing additional training as needed. Share the lessons learned openly with the team, highlighting how the organization is becoming more resilient as a result. Recognize and reward individuals who contribute valuable insights and take the initiative to implement changes. This encourages a culture where learning is valued and everyone has a role to play in the improvement.

While the pressure of a crisis can make it tempting to just focus on survival, learning leaders know that taking the time to reflect and improve set their organization up for greater success in the long run. By embracing the act of learning, you can turn the challenges of a crisis into opportunities for growth, enhancing your skills and the resilience of your team. The more you prioritize learning, the better equipped youll be to navigate future crises with confidence and agility. Learning is about more than just recovering from a crisis–it's about emerging stronger and more capable on the other side.

10. Consistency

Last, but certainly not least, we have consistency, which provides a sense of stability and predictability, even in the midst of chaos. When leaders respond to a crisis in a consistent manner, it helps stakeholders understand what to expect and how to navigate the situation. This clarity will help reduce anxiety and confusion, enabling people to focus on the tasks at hand. Consistency is also another one of the "10 keys" that builds trust. When words and actions align, stakeholders feel that leaders are reliable and truthful. This trust is crucial for maintaining credibility and cooperation during a crisis. Consistency extends to messaging, decision-making processes, and behavior. Ensure that communication across all channels and from all leaders conveys the same key information and tone. Establish clear criteria for decision-making, and apply those criteria consistently. This transparency helps stakeholders understand the reasoning behind actions, even if they may disagree with the specific decisions.

But don't let a commitment to consistency keep you from being flexible. You still must be able to adapt to changing circumstances and adjust plans as necessary. However, when pivoting, strive to maintain consistency in core values, messaging, and expectations. This provides an anchor for stakeholders amidst the shifts. Lead by example, and demonstrate consistent behaviors and standards that you expect from others. This helps create a culture where consistency is valued at all levels. Leaders must be mindful of the example they're setting and the messages they're sending, even in the heat of the moment.

CASE STUDIES

Now we are going to dive into a few real-world case studies. We will look at one bad and one good example.

In April 2010, the Deepwater Horizon drilling rig explosion created the largest marine oil spill in history [30], resulting in eleven deaths, seventeen injuries, and unprecedented environmental damage. The subsequent crisis response offers critical lessons in corporate responsibility and public relations.

As oil poured into the Gulf of Mexico for several weeks, the oil devastated marine ecosystems, local fisheries and coastal communities. British Petroleum (hereafter referred to as BP), who was the company that was funding the drilling operation, initiated response measures to contain the damage, but their efforts proved insufficient and poorly coordinated.

Their crisis management strategy unfolded in three distinct phases, each marked by significant missteps. Initially, BP attempted to deflect responsibility to their contractors [31]. When this approach failed to minimize public outcry, they then shifted their focus to downplaying the severity of the spill by significantly underreporting the spill volume. Their estimates of roughly 1,000 barrels of oil per day (42,000 gallons) [32] spilling into the Gulf sharply contrasted with the actual volume of the spill, which varied between 12,000-19,000 barrels per day (504,000-798,000 gallons) [33]. The revelation of this discrepancy severely undermined BP's credibility during the crisis and further damaged their image.

In their third phase of the crisis response, BP launched an extensive public relations campaign. Between April and July 2010, while oil continued to contaminate the Gulf, the company allocated $93 million to advertising campaigns focused on public apology [33]. Instead of spending an almost nine figure sum on cleaning up the damage, BP was more focused on attempting to clean up their image. This, once again, drew even more criticism from the public and shareholders.

The situation deteriorated further when BP CEO Tony Hayward gave an infamous interview with a British newspaper. In the interview, Hayward commented on the emotional impact of the disaster, saying "I'd like my life back" [35]. These insensitive remarks were perceived as dismissive of the suffering caused by the spill, and of course, of the eleven workers who tragically lost their life.

Less than a month after this comment, he was photographed taking a trip on his yacht [36].

There were multiple communication failures by BP, in both the response and recovery stages. The first misstep was to shift blame to the contractors. This was a fundamental holding statement failure, as, like we went through earlier, you cannot point fingers in a holding statement.

The next misstep was downplaying the severity of the spill, by grossly understating the amount of oil spilling in the Gulf. This lack of transparency, honesty, and accountability greatly deteriorated public trust, as well as BP's reputation.

The third issue stemmed from BP entering the recovery stage too early. BP spent $93 million on advertising to restore public trust and improve the company's reputation. But by jumping into the recovery stage before the oil spill had been fully dealt with, BP instead faced widespread public outcry which only further damaged their image.

The next failures came from Tony Hayward. From his comment on wanting his life back, to his vacation while the disaster raged on, we can easily understand why these mistakes only amplified public outcry.

While very few men and women in history will ever have to face a corporate crisis like BP and its CEO Tony Hayward did, we know not to make the egregious communicative mistakes that they made during the disaster.

Now let's shift our focus to the good example of crisis management. For this, we will go back to 1982 to look at how Johnson & Johnson handled the Tylenol tampering case.

Back in 1982, Tylenol was the leading over-the-counter painkiller in the United States, accounting for 37% of the industry market share [37].

Then, in the fall of 1982, for reasons still unknown, an unknown person decided to tamper with bottles of Tylenol by lacing extra-strength capsules with nearly three times the fatal cyanide dosage, re-sealing the bottles, and placing them back on the shelves of multiple pharmacies and grocery stores in the Chicago area [38]. Soon after, seven consumers were dead from the laced capsules.

It didn't take long for Chicago police to find the link between the laced bottles and the seven victims. And just like that, Johnson & Johnson had a crisis they had no hand in creating.

So how do you handle a public health crisis that isn't your company's fault? You could shift the blame to the individuals responsible, saving millions of bottles from being recalled and protecting your bottom line, or, you could realize that regardless of fault, this is a public health crisis, and recall *thirty-one million bottles* of Tylenol to protect from further deaths.

Johnson & Johnson chose the latter.

Over $100,000,000 worth of Tylenol was immediately recalled, and Johnson and Johnson issued an alert to consumers not to consume the product. They offered to exchange existing bottles for safe ones, once again, showing the company's commitment to protecting public safety over profits.

But Johnson and Johnson wasn't done yet, within six weeks, they had designed the first ever triple-lock tamper-resistant container [39], the first of its kind. This technology would soon become the industry norm, and would even later be used in other industries as well in order to protect consumers.

Johnson & Johnson's immediate response, which put public health over profits, showed empathy, transparency, timeliness and honesty. This crisis response ensured that Johnson & Johnson regained public trust in record time, and as a result, Tylenol went back to its original market share within a year of the crisis.

There are several takeaways from the crisis response in both of these high-profile cases.

Prioritizing safety versus prioritizing profits

In the Tylenol case, Johnson & Johnson immediately prioritized public safety over profits by recalling thirty-one million bottles of Tylenol, and taking a massive $100,000,000 hit in the process. They realized that ensuring public safety was paramount, and the response regained public trust. As for BP p.l.c., the initial finger-pointing to their contractors and subsequent downplaying of the size of the oil spill in order to protect share prices broke public trust and led to widespread criticism.

Swift action versus foot dragging

Johnson & Johnson's swift and decisive action of issuing a product recall within a single week and designing new tamper-proof packaging in the following weeks, led to increased public trust and respect of the company. BP's slow action to contain the spill was harmful to both the environment and BP's public image.

Back to normalcy versus prolonged effects

Due to Johnson & Johnson's immediate and effective action, and by putting empathy, transparency, timeliness, and honesty first, Tylenol was able to retake its dominant market share less than a year after the crisis. BP on the other hand, permanently damaged its image because of its ineffectual response. The damage to the Gulf and the local communities are still being felt today, with a permanent stain on BP's brand image that it will never be able to shake.

CHAPTER 14

Building a Culture of Effective Communication

The art of communication is the language of leadership.
-James Humes

Building a thriving organization isn't merely about strategic planning and efficient operations, it's fundamentally about *people*. And the lifeblood of connecting those people, driving collaboration, fostering innovation, and ultimately, determining success, is communication. And as we have learned in these pages, it's more than sending emails or giving some feedback in a meeting. It's about creating a culture where open, honest, and respectful communication flows freely at all levels. And that starts with *you*, the leader. You have to instill that culture and cultivate that mindset in those who follow. Imagine an orchestra for a second. At an individual level, each musician in the orchestra is one of the best at what they do, but without a conductor to lead them, the result is chaos, not harmony. Similarly, in any organization, whether it be a nonprofit or a fortune 500 company, a well orchestrated communication system is what drives the organization to success. It is the driving factor in bringing out the best in each team member, and creating that harmony. Building such a system requires a deliberate and sustained effort, a conscious decision to prioritize communication as a core value.

BUILDING A CULTURE OF EFFECTIVE COMMUNICATION

The first crucial element in building this culture is instilling psychological safety. This means creating an environment where individuals feel comfortable expressing their opinions, sharing concerns, and even admitting mistakes without fear or retribution. This isn't about eliminating accountability though, it is about separating the message from the messenger. When team members feel safe voicing concerns, the organization gains a valuable early warning system for potential problems, fostering proactive problem solving instead of reactive firefighting.

Consider a scenario of a software development team. If developers are afraid to report bugs or suggest alternative approaches for fear of criticism, the final product will inevitably suffer. However, if a culture of psychological safety is in place, where honest feedback is encouraged and valued, the team can identify and address issues early, leading to a superior product and a more efficient development process.

Transparency is another cornerstone of a communicative culture. This means being open about organizational goals, challenges, and decisions. Keeping employees in the dark breeds mistrust and resentment. Regular, honest updates, even about difficult situations, demonstrates respect and fosters a sense of ownership and commitment. This transparency isn't about oversharing every detail though. Just provide enough relevant information to keep team members informed and involved. For instance, during a period of restructuring, transparent communication can alleviate anxiety and speculation by providing clear explanations of the reasons behind the changes and their potential impact on employees. Open communication channels, such as regular meetings, employee surveys, and easily accessible internal communication platforms, can help facilitate this transparency.

Effective feedback mechanisms are also vital. In addition to regular performance reviews, you should build a system of continuous feedback. This can include regular check-ins between managers and team members, as well as 360 degree feedback. This is a type of feedback where team members receive anonymous feedback from subordinates, managers, peers, stockholders, customers, as well as themselves. The idea is to get feedback from individuals all around the person, hence the term 360 degree feedback.

According to a study from *Forbes*, more than 85% of Fortune 500 companies use 360 degree feedback as a cornerstone of their leadership development process [40].

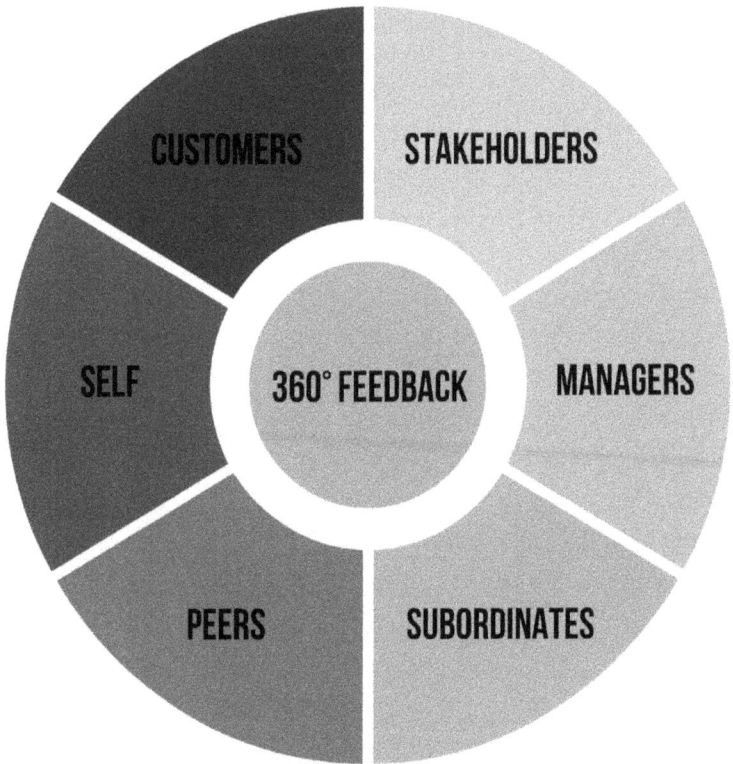

Both of these tools can provide valuable insights and help individuals improve their own communication skills and performance. This requires a shift away from feedback as a judgmental tool to feedback as a developmental one, focusing on growth and improvement rather than blame. Remember, it's about creating a safe space for honest conversations about performance, both positive and negative, facilitating a cycle of continuous improvement and professional growth.

Training and development are also essential to building a culture of communication. Providing employees with the skills and tools they need to communicate effectively is vital. This can include workshops on active listening, effective communication techniques, conflict resolution, and intercultural communication. Regular training reinforces the importance of communication and provides employees with practical skills they can immediately apply in their work. Investing in communication skills training sends a clear message that the organization values communication and is committed to helping employees develop this crucial skill set.

You need to also lead by example. Leaders must embody the communication culture they wish to see in their organization. They should be active listeners, provide constructive feedback, and proactively seek input from their teams. Your communication will set the tone for the entire organization to follow. If leaders are consistently dismissive of feedback, avoid difficult conversations that need to occur, or just generally communicate poorly, their teams will not embrace a culture of open and honest communication. Authenticity is key, team members can easily spot disingenuous attempts to foster communication. Leaders must exemplify the traits they wish to see from others.

Furthermore, the organization's communication infrastructure should be carefully considered. This could include an internal communication platform that facilitates quick and efficient messaging, allows for document sharing, and encourages collaboration between team members. Consider also implementing regular newsletter or updates to keep team members informed on organizational news, achievements, and upcoming events. You can also use this newsletter to highlight individual employee achievements as a way to motivate your team.

The effectiveness of this communicative culture should be regularly reviewed. This can be done through employee surveys, behavioral observation, or simply asking team members how they feel about the communication of their team or the organization as a whole. Gathering feedback will give you a crystal clear view of areas for improvements, as well as what has been done well in the current system. It also will ensure that the communication strategies are aligned with the organization's goals and the needs of its employees. The evaluation process should b e transparent and involve input from all levels of the organization. If you decide to use surveys, make sure to track the responses in a spreadsheet to easily identify areas for improvement. You should also make sure to use the same survey year after year (minor tweaks may be necessary) to ensure that you can pinpoint improvements year after year. Using data to track communication effectiveness allows for adjustments and refinements to the communication strategy, ensuring it remains relevant and effective over time.

SUSTAINING A CULTURE OF EFFECTIVE COMMUNICATION

The orchestra of success, as we've established, relies on a conductor–a leader–who expertly orchestrates communication. But even the most gifted conductor needs continuous practice, refinement, and a willingness to learn. Leadership communication, much like any other skill, isn't static. It's a dynamic evolving art. The business world is in perpetual motion, a whirlwind of technological advancements, shifting market trends, and evolving societal expectations. Leaders who fail to adapt, risk becoming out of tune with their organization and its environment. Stagnation is a sure path to irrelevance.

Think of now seasoned CEOs who started their careers in an era of fax machines and landlines. Their communication styles, honed over years of practice, are less effective i n today's world of instant messaging, social media, and virtual collab oration. They had to adapt to a changing world of business in order to stay on top. They had to learn how to effectively communicate across diverse digital platforms, understanding the nuances of each channel. Perhaps they had to grasp how to leverage social media for organizational story-telling and engagement. The point is, their initial skill set, while valuable at one time, needed to change and adapt to stay relevant and effective.

But this is more about simply keeping up, leaders need to proactively anticipate changes and need to position themself at the forefront of communication best practices. A commitment to lifelong learning allows leaders to not only maintain their effectiveness, but also to expand their communication repertoire, exploring new and innovative ways to connect with their teams and stakeholders.

The journey of continuous learning can take many forms. Formal training programs offer structured learning experiences with expert guidance. These could involve workshops on public speaking, negotiation skills, or conflict resolution. Executive coaching, another effective strategy, provides personalized support and guidance, tailored to the specific needs and challenges of the individual leader. A skilled coach can provide valuable feedback, identify blind spots, and help leaders develop strategies to overcome communication obstacles.

But formal learning isn't the only path. Informal learning plays a vital role as well. Actively seeking feedback from colleagues, subordinates and superiors, can provide a holistic perspective on one's communication strengths and weaknesses. Informal learning also includes reading materials centered on leadership communication (congratulations, you're doing this right now), as well as attending industry conferences, or even listening to podcasts or YouTube videos featuring communication experts. It also includes observing effective communicators both inside and outside your organization.

Analyze their approaches–what techniques do they employ? How do they build rapport with their audience? What strategies do they utilize to overcome communication barriers? By actively observing and analyzing, you can learn valuable insights and adapt successful strategies into your own communicative arsenal.

It is also crucial to understand that this continuous improvement cycle isn't linear, it's iterative. You'll make mistakes, face challenges, and experience setbacks along the way. The key is to embrace these experiences as learning opportunities. Conduct regular self-assessments, analyzing your successes and failures to identify areas for improvement. This process should be proactive and self-directed, driven by a genuine desire to enhance one's communication abilities and contribute to the organization's overall success.

The Last Word

You've made it to the end of this book, but your journey as an effective communicator is just beginning.

Great communication isn't about perfection. It's about presence. It's about showing up as yourself, speaking with clarity, leading with confidence, and listening like someone's career depends on it (because that might just be the case).

The best leaders don't sound like they're reading from a handbook. They sound like *themselves*. They've learned how to turn down the volume of the negative voices in their head, and turn up their natural voice. They know when to lean into vulnerability, and when to stand firm in their conviction.

We wrote this book for two main types of people; those who want to learn to communicate like a leader, and those who want to hone their skills further. If you are the former, you may be wondering *"do I have what it takes to lead?"*

You do.

The very fact that you picked up this book, and made it to the end proves that you care enough to grow. That's better than some people in management positions already.

Will you make mistakes? Absolutely. But a leader is not a perfect, faultless individual, a leader is an individual who learns from their mistakes and doesn't repeat them. They bounce back stronger. Every. Single. Time.

Recover, learn, move forward. That's how you lead. Think of how a great quarterback leads their team. The best in the business aren't perfect. They throw interceptions, fumble the ball, get sacked. But they don't give in. When a quarterback throws an interception, they'll immediately shift to defense to keep the opposing player from running it back for a score. *Recovery.* Then, they go to the sideline, pick up the tablet, and watch the film. "What did I do wrong? Was it the throw? Did I misread the coverage? Was there a defensive back I didn't see?" *Learn.* Then they go back out there, better than before, because now they know how to avoid making the same mistake again. *Move Forward.*

The best quarterbacks in the business score the next drive.

As a leader, you must be willing to make mistakes, and learn from them. For some that's a scary thing, but you must think of it as an *opportunity* to get better. If you truly want to be great at what you do, you cannot shy away from that.

This relentless pursuit of self-improvement, this unwavering commitment to learning and adaptation, is not a solitary endeavor. Surround yourself with individuals who challenge you, who offer honest feedback, and who celebrate your victories alongside you. Seek mentors who have walked the path you aspire to lead, and be equally willing to mentor those who are just beginning their own journey. Build a network of trusted advisors, colleagues, and friends who can provide diverse perspectives and support you through inevitable challenges. Build a strong foundation of relationships and empower others to rise with you. Your communication skills, refined and honed through continuous effort and growth, will be your most powerful tool in forging these connections and cultivating a culture of shared growth.

As a leader, every conversation is a chance to build trust, every email is an opportunity to show someone that you care, and every meeting is a moment to move people toward a shared vision. It is up to you to make the most of these opportunities, and become the leader you've always wanted to be.

References

Chapter 1

[1] J. M. Kilner., & R. N. Lemon. (2013, December 2). *What we know currently about mirror neurons.* National Library of Medicine-https://pubmed.ncbi.nlm.nih.gov/24309286/

[2] X. Gu, Z. Gao, X. Wang, X. Liu, R. T. Knight, P. R. Hof, & J. Fan. (2012, September). *Anterior insular cortex is necessary for empathetic pain perception.* National Library of Medicine https://doi.org/10.1093/brain/aws199

Chapter 2

[3] S. Rathje, L. Hackel, & J. Zaki. (2021, July). *Attending live theatre improves empathy, changes attitudes, and leads to pro-social behavior.* Journal of Experimental Social Psychology. https://www.sciencedirect.com/science/article/abs/pii/S002210312100038X

[4] K. Gurchiek. (2016, April 18). *Survey: Respect at work boosts job satisfaction.* Society for Human Resource Management. https://www.shrm.org/topics-tools/news/employee-relations/survey-respect-work-boosts-job-satisfaction

[5] S. H. Kwon. (2024). *Analyzing the impact of team-building interventions on team cohesion in sports teams: a meta-analysis study.* Frontiers in Psychology, 15, 1353944. https://doi.org/10.3389/fpsyg.2024.1353944

Chapter 3

[6] Perceptyx. (2022, April 26). *Employers that act on worker feedback are 3x as likely to hit financial targets.* GlobeNewswire NewsRoom. https://blog.perceptyx.com/news-employers-that-act-on-worker-feedback-are-3x-as-likely-to-hit-financial-targets#:~:text=TEMECULA%2C%20Calif.%2C%20April%2026,of%20customer%20satisfaction%20and%20retention.

Chapter 4

[7] J. Willis, & A. Todorov. (2006, July). *First Impressions: Making up your mind after a 100-MS exposure to a face.* Sage Journals. https://journals.sagepub.com/doi/10.1111/j.1467-9280.2006.01750.x

[8] A. Mehrabian. (1981). *Silent messages: Implicit communication of emotions and attitudes.* Wadsworth Pub. Co.

[9] D. Gatica-Perez. (2009, January 16). *Automatic nonverbal analysis of social interaction in small groups: A review.* Science Direct. https://www.sciencedirect.com/science/article/abs/pii/S0262885609000109

[10] N. Zandan. (2013, June 27). *Eye Contact – A Declining Communications Tool?* Quantified AI. https://www.quantified.ai/blog/eye-contact-a-declining-communications-tool/

[11] V. Van Edwards. (2024, June 13). *60 hand gestures you should be using and their meaning.* Science of People. https://www.scienceofpeople.com/hand-gestures/

[12] M. Koppensteiner, P. Stephan., & J. P. M. Jäschke. (2015, October). *More than words: Judgments of politicians and the role of different communication channels.* Journal of Research in Personality. https://www.sciencedirect.com/science/article/pii/S0092656615000550

[13] M. Koppensteiner, P. Stephan., & J. P. M. Jäschke. (2015, February). *From body motion to cheers: Speakers' body movements as predictors of applause.* Personality and Individual Differences. https://www.sciencedirect.com/science/article/pii/S0191886914005832

[14] T. L. Chartrand, & J. A. Bargh. (1999). *The chameleon effect: the perception-behavior link and social interaction.* Journal of personality and social psychology, 76(6), 893–910. https://doi.org/10.1037//0022-3514.76.6.893

[15] J. Kwak. (2015, July 24). *What your body language says about your leadership skills.* GovLoop. https://www.govloop.com/community/blog/body-language-says-leadership-skills/

[16] Y. Shah. (2024, September 27). *Is fidgeting a sign of a mental health condition?.* NOCD. https://www.treatmyocd.com/what-is-ocd/info/related-symptoms-conditions/is-fidgeting-a-sign-of-a-mental-health-condition#

[17] A. Escalona. (2025, February 24). *How hand gestures reflect the speaker's personality traits - aryo consulting group.* Aryo Consulting Group - Strategy and Small Business Consulting. https://aryocg.com/how-hand-gestures-reflect-the-speakers-personality-traits/#:~:text=For%20starters%2C%20when%20speakers%20express,presence%20of%20hostility%20or%20aggression.

[18] A. Kandola. (2020, April 26). *Dilated pupils meaning: Attraction and mood.* Medical News Today. https://www.medicalnewstoday.com/articles/dilated-pupils-meaning

[19] A. I. Korda, G. Giannakakis, E. Ventouras, P. A. Asvestas, N. Smyrnis, K. Marias, & G. K. Matsopoulos. (2021). *Recognition of Blinks Activity Patterns during Stress Conditions Using CNN and Markovian Analysis.* Signals, 2(1), 55-71. https://doi.org/10.3390/signals2010006

[20] Department of Health & Human Services. (2014, October 2). *Breathing to reduce stress.* Better Health Channel. https://www.betterhealth.vic.gov.au/health/healthyliving/breathing-to-reduce-stress

Chapter 5

[21] A. Heeren, G. Ceschi, DP. Valentiner, V. Dethier, P. Philippot. (2013, May 3). *Assessing public speaking fear with the short form of the Personal Report of Confidence as a Speaker scale: confirmatory factor analyses among a French-speaking community sample.* Neuropsychiatr Dis Treat. https://pubmed.ncbi.nlm.nih.gov/23662060/

[22] A. García-Monge, S. Guijarro-Romero, E. Santamaría-Vázquez, L. Martínez-Álvarez, N. Bores-Calle. (2023, November 27). *Embodied strategies for public speaking anxiety: evaluation of the Corp-Oral program.* Front Hum Neurosci. https://pmc.ncbi.nlm.nih.gov/articles/PMC10711069/

Chapter 6

[23] A. H. Maslow. (1943). *A theory of human motivation.* Psychological Review, 50(4), 370–396.

[24] F. Herzberg. (1964). *The motivation-hygiene concept and problems of manpower.* Personnel Administration, 27(1), 3–7.

[25] E. A. Locke, & G. P. Latham. (1990). *A theory of goal setting & task performance.* Prentice-Hall, Inc.

[26] V. Vroom. (1964). *Expectancy Theory.*

[27] J. S. Adams. (1963) *Toward an Understanding of Inequity.* Journal of Abnormal and Social Psychology, 67, 422-436.

Chapter 7

[28] I. B. Myers. (1962). *The Myers-Briggs Type Indicator: Manual (1962).* Consulting Psychologists Press.

Chapter 8

[29] G. H. Seijts, & D. Crim. (2006). What engages employees the most or, the Ten C's of employee engagement. *Ivey Business Journal, 70*(4), 1-5.

[30] M. McDonald. (2018, January 3). *Do your measures make employees mad? or motivate them?* Gallup. https://www.gallup.com/workplace/231659/performance-measures-motivate-madden-employees.aspx#:~:text=Measurement%20used%20in%20the%20right%20way%20is%20motivating.&text=Measurement%20used%20in%20the%20wrong,quali-fied%20to%20judge%20their%20performance.

Chapter 9

[31] S. Scott. (2012, June). *The Learning Habits of Leaders and Managers.* Amazon AWS. https://s3-eu-west-1.amazonaws.com/goodpractice-marketing/GoodPractice+Insights+June+2012.pdf

Chapter 10

[32] U.S. Bureau of Labor Statistics. (2023, September 28). *One out of five workers teleworked in August 2023.* U.S. Bureau of Labor Statistics. https://www.bls.gov/opub/ted/2023/one-out-of-five-workers-teleworked-in-august-2023.htm#:~:text=About%20one%20in%20five%20(19.5,October%202022%20and%20August%202023.

Chapter 11

[33] *Managing Across Distance in Today's Economic Climate.* (April 20, 2016). Harvard Business Review Analytic Services.
Managing Across Distance in Today's Economic Climate

Chapter 12

[34] R. Fisher, & W. Ury. (1981). *Getting to yes: negotiating agreement without giving in.* Boston, Houghton Mifflin.

Chapter 13

[35] National Oceanic and Atmospheric Administration. (2024, July 8). *What have been the largest oil spills in U.S. history?* NOAA. https://oceanservice.noaa.gov/education/tutorial-coastal/oil-spills/os02.html

[36] E. Shogren. (2011, April 21). *BP: A textbook example of how not to handle Pr.* NPR. https://www.npr.org/2011/04/21/135575238/bp-a-textbook-example-of-how-not-to-handle-pr

[37] R. Pallardy. (2024, October 23). *Deepwater Horizon Oil Spill.* Encyclopædia Britannica. https://www.britannica.com/event/Deepwater-Horizon-oil-spill

[38] E. Martinez. (2020, September 8). *British Petroleum Deepwater Horizon Oil Spill Case.* Rights Of Nature Tribunal. https://www.rightsofnatureribunal.org/cases/british-petroleum-deepwater-horizon-oil-spill-case/

[39] Associated Press. (2010, September 2). *BP spent $93M on advertising after Gulf Spill.* CBS News. https://www.cbsnews.com/news/bp-spent-93m-on-advertising-after-gulf-spill/

[40] Reuters. (2010, June 2). *BP CEO apologizes for "thoughtless" oil spill comment | Reuters.* https://www.reuters.com/article/oil-spill-bp-apology/bp-ceo-apologizes-for-thoughtless-oil-spill-comment-idUSN0217664920100602/

[41] BBC. (2010, June 20). *BP CEO Tony Hayward criticised for Yacht Trip.* BBC News. https://www.bbc.com/news/10359120

[42] *Case Study: The Johnson & Johnson Tylenol Crisis.* Oklahoma University. (n.d.). https://www.ou.edu/deptcomm/dodjcc/groups/02C2/Johnson%20&%20Johnson.htm

[43] C. Gutowski, & S. St. Clair. (2024, June 14). *The tylenol murders: The story of a 40-year-old unsolved case begins with a terrifying medical mystery.* Chicago Tribune. https://www.chicagotribune.com/2022/09/22/the-tylenol-murders-the-story-of-a-40-year-old-unsolved-case-begins-with-a-terrifying-medical-mystery/

[44] A. Caesar-Gordon. (2021, April 30). *The perfect crisis response?.* PR Week. https://www.prweek.com/article/1357203/perfect-crisis-response

Chapter 14

[45] J. Zenger. (2016, March 10). *How effective are your 360-degree feedback assessments?* Forbes. https://www.forbes.com/sites/jackzenger/2016/03/10/how-effective-are-your-360-degree-feedback-assessments/

Further Reading

Articles:

M. Koppensteiner, P. Stephan, & J. P. M. Jäschke. (2015, February). *From body motion to cheers: Speakers' body movements as predictors of applause.* Personality and Individual Differences.

https://www.sciencedirect.com/science/article/pii/S0191886914005832

If you are interested in a more academic perspective on the relationship between nonverbal cues and audience response, this is a very well-researched analytical study. We briefly looked into this study in chapter four, but reading it in its entirety is well worth the read. It provides valuable insights into the power of nonverbal communication on the basis of influencing audience reaction and engagement.

V. Van Edwards. (2024, June 13). *60 hand gestures you should be using and their meaning.* Science of People.

https://www.scienceofpeople.com/hand-gestures/

For those eager to delve deeper into the fascinating science of nonverbal communication and its impact on interpersonal interactions, consider looking into this comprehensive guide. This resource offers a detailed exploration into various hand gestures, elucidating their meanings and providing a practical guide for effective use.

Books:

A. Mehrabian. (1981). *Silent messages: Implicit communication of emotions and attitudes.* Wadsworth Pub. Co.

Possibly Albert Mehrabian's most well known book, *Silent Messages* was where the 55-38-7 rule of communication originated. This work has been out of print for a few decades now, so physical copies aren't easy to come by, but you can find pdf copies of the book online for free.

D. Ramsey. (2011). *EntreLeadership: 20 Years of Practical Business Wisdom from the Trenches.* Howard Books.

This book provides a practical framework for business leaders, emphasizing key principles such as disciplined financial management, creating a strong company culture, effective hiring and firing practices, and the importance of clear communication. Ramsey's approach is rooted in his own experience building and running successful organizations.

E. A. Locke, & G. P. Latham. (1990). *A theory of goal setting & task performance.* Prentice-Hall, Inc.

This influential work details the principles of goal-setting theory, empathizing the importance of goal specificity, difficulty, feedback, and commitment in driving task performance. Locke and Latham's research demonstrates that well-defined, challenging goals consistently result in improved outcomes.

L. Babin & J. Willink. (2015). *Extreme Ownership: How U.S. Navy Seals Lead and Win.* St. Martin's Press.

Written by two former U.S. Navy Seals, this book applies the lessons learned in high-pressure combat situations to the challenges faced by leaders in any field. *Extreme Ownership* promotes a mindset of accountability and proactive problem-solving, offering a unique perspective on leadership development.

V. Vroom. (1964). *Expectancy Theory.* Wiley.

This work presents the foundational Expectancy Theory, a core model in motivational psychology. Vroom's work explores how individual's beliefs about effort, performance, and rewards influence their motivation. Essential reading for understanding the cognitive processes driving workplace behavior.